St Brides Wentloog Church

THE OLD PARISH CHURCHES OF GWENT, GLAMORGAN & GOWER
Mike Salter

CONTENTS

A GLOSSARY OF TERMS

Apse	- Semi-circular or polygonal east end of a church containing an altar.
Ashlar	- Masonry of blocks with even faces and square edges.
Broaches	- Sloping half pyramids adapting an octagonal spire to a square tower.
Cable Moulding	- Norman moulding imitating a twisted cord.
Chancel	- The eastern part of a church used by the clergy.
Chevron Ornament	- Norman ornament with a continuous series of Vs forming a zig-zag.
Clerestorey	- The upper storey of the nave of a church, pierced by windows.
Collar Beam	- A tie-beam used higher up nearer the apex of a roof.
Corbel	- A projecting bracket supporting a wall, image, or beam.
Corbel Table	- A continuous row of corbels supporting a parapet.
Crossing Tower	- A tower built upon four arches in the middle of a cruciform church.
Cruciform Church	- A cross-shaped church with transepts forming the arms of the cross.
Cusp	- A projecting point between the foils in a foiled Gothic arch.
Decorated	- A division of English Gothic architecture roughly from 1290 to 1360.
Dog Tooth	- Four cornered stars placed diagonally and raised pyramidally.
Early English	- The first division of English Gothic architecture from 1200 to 1290.
Elizabethan	- Of the time of Queen Elizabeth I (1558-1603).
Embattled	- Provided with a series of indentations (crenels).
Fleuron	- Rectilinear flower or leaf carved in low relief.
Foil	- A lobe formed by the cusping of a circle or an arch.
Four Centered Arch	- A low, flattish arch with each curve drawn from two compass points.
Hagioscope	- (Squint) A hole cut in a wall to allow a view of the high altar.
Head Stops	- Heads of humans or beasts forming the ends of a hoodmould.
Herringbone Masonry	- Courses of stones alternately sloping at 45 degrees to horizontal.
Hoodmould	- A projecting moulding above an arch or lintel to throw off water.
Impost	- A wall bracket, often moulded, to support the end of an arch.
Jacobean	- Of the time of King James I (1603-25).
Jamb	- The side of a doorway, window, or other opening.
Lancet	- A long, comparatively narrow window usually with a pointed head.
Light	- A compartment of a window.
Miserichord	- Bracket underneath hinged choir stall seat to support standing person.
Mullion	- A vertical member dividing the lights of a window.
Nave	- The part of a church in which the congregation sits.
Norman	- Division of English Romanesque architecture from 1066 to c1200.
Ogival Arch	- Arch of oriental origin with both convex and concave curves.
Perpendicular	- A division of English Gothic architecture from c1360 to 1540.
Pilaster	- Flat buttress or pier attached to a wall. Used in the Norman period.
Piscina	- A stone basin used for rinsing out holy vessels after a Mass.
Plinth	- The projecting base of a wall.
Quoins	- The dressed stones at the corners of a building.
Rere-Arch	- The arch on the inside face of a window embrasure or doorway.
Respond	- A half-pier or column bonded into a wall, and carrying an arch.
Reticulation	- Tracery with a netlike appeerence.
Rood Screen	- A screen with a crucifix mounted upon it between a nave and chancel.
Sedilia	- The seats for priests (usually three) on the south side of a chancel.
Soffit	- The underside of an arch or lintel.
Spandrel	- The surface between two arches.
Tie-Beam	- A beam connecting the slopes of a roof at or near its foot.
Tracery	- The intersecting ribwork in the upper part of a later Gothic window.
Tympanum	- The space between the lintel of a doorway and the arch above it.
Victorian	- Of the time of Queen Victoria (1837-1901).
Wall Plate	- A timber laid longitudinally along the top of a wall.
Windbraces	- The struts used to strengthen the sloping sides of a roof.

Doorway,
St Hilary

Chancel arch,
Runston

Herringbone masonry at Old Cogan

INTRODUCTION

Christianity was well established in Wales by the 6th century but little remains of churches or their contents prior to the late 11th century Norman invasion. In Gwent and Glamorgan there are just the fine crosses and grave slabs at Llantwit Major, Margam, and a few other places, and foundations on Barry Island of a tiny rectangular chapel of uncertain date with an east apse for an altar. By the 9th century Wales contained a number of monastic mother churches (Clas) which each administered several small chapels-of-ease. The latter may have mostly been of wood or unmortared stone, but eventually all the mother churches had mortared stone walls with tiny round arched openings and thatched roofs. However subsequent enlargements and rebuildings have left no standing remains of any in South Wales.

By 1100 the Normans founded Benedictine priories at Monmouth, Chepstow, Cardiff, and Abergavenny, and those of Usk and Ewenny followed by 1140. Gradually these put up stone churches. Ruination or rebuilding has removed much early work but Chepstow retains the arcades of an aisled nave, Ewenny part of an unaisled nave, and Usk a central tower. Townsfolk worshipped in the naves of these churches and ensured their survival after the monasteries were dissolved in 1535-40. Cardiff Prior was later destroyed by river erosion. Of the village churches there is walling with herringbone masonry at Old Cogan and Dixton, a tall narrow doorway at St Hilary and naves at Llandegfedd and Newport, the latter now serving as a chapel.

From c1150 to 1200 there was a boom in church building. Almost all the existing churches were rebuilt or extended and many fresh churches erected, many of them in conjunction with nearby castles. More than a tenth of the 230 medieval churches in Glamorgan and Gwent retain a central core of this period or they have openings either in or ex-situ, or fonts. Runston has a typical small chapel of this period. The congregation would have stood on a rush covered earth floor in a rectangular nave with a thatch roof and whitewashed internal walls decorated with simple motifs painted mostly in red, yellow and black. Later these developed into murals of scenes from the lives of Christ and the saints. There were two doorways and two tiny round arched windows with deep internal splayed openings. Through a plain round arch in the east wall the congregation could look into the chancel, a square room lighted with two windows and just big enough to contain the altar and an attendant priest. There are much rebuilt aisled naves of c1150 at Newport and Margam. Several churches have towers probably of c1150-1200 but only at Llancarfan do original two-light belfry openings survive later remodelling.

3

Coychurch Church

In Wales it was not very common for medieval congregations to increase sufficiently to warrant enlarging the nave of a church, usually by adding on aisles. In Glamorgan an aisle had been added at Llancarfan by c1200, and in the late 13th century Llantwit Major and Coyrchurch were rebuilt with two side aisles, but in the later medieval period aisles were only added at Cardiff, St Andrews Major, Cowbridge (where the aisle replaced a chapel-of-ease) and perhaps Llanthrithyd. Aisles are only slightly more common in Gwent, dating from the 13th century at Skenfrith and Grosmont, where there were major castles close at hand, from the 14th century at Mitchel Troy, Trelleck, and Llantilio Crucorney (the latter two were again near castles), and from the 15th century at Magor, Peterstone Wentloog, Redwick, Christchurch, and a few other churches.

Towers, on the other hand, are common in South Wales churches. Over two thirds of the churches of Gwent and Glamorgan possessed something more substantial than a simple bell-cote on the west wall by the 1540s, and an even higher proportion had a stone porch. The towers mostly stand against the west wall of the nave, but about a dozen or so lie in a central position between the nave and chancel with or without flanking transepts. Transepts do occasionally occur without a central tower, as at Llanblethian. They provided space for subsidiary altars and often also contained niches for tombs of benefactors. In the rare instances of a tower lying in a transeptal position, as at Ilston and St Mellons, the lowest storey formed a chapel with an altar. Medieval vestries are uncommon but survive at Combridge, Llantwit Major, Llysworney, and Trelleck.

4

Aumbry, Trelleck

Sedilia at St Fagans

Llancarfan Church

The building boom begun in c1150 slowed down in the early 14th century, and the ravages of plague finally stopped work in c1350. In the 1190s the pointed arch began to appear in chancel arches and was gradually adopted also for arcades, windows, and doorways. More than half the churches of Gwent and Glamorgan have masonry of the period 1200-1300. Only Grosmont and Skenfrith are of note in Gwent and Coychurch, Llantwit Major, Llysworney, Cowbridge, and Cheriton (all of these have central towers) in Glamorgan. Usually the work is plain and has subsequently been altered or restored. Chancels of this period are larger than before (choirs were gradually coming into fashion and required space) and have a separate doorway.

During the late 13th century the single lancet lights used from c1200 onwards were sometimes given cusped heads and placed together in pairs. Eventually the spandrel between the arch heads would be pierced as at Llangwm Uchaf and Llanvapley and so tracery evolved. The elaborate floral and geometrical designs of tracery that are typical in England in c1290-1360 rarely flourished in the village churches of Wales where work of that period is rarely distinguished. Window tracery in the aisled naves at Trelleck and Mitchel Troy, in the unaisled Gower churches of Rhossili, Pennard, and Penmaen (all these replaced Norman churches engulfed by sand-dunes) and in the aisle and chapel at Llancarfan is simple or absent altogether. The cruciform churches at Coity and St Georges are more notable. There are spires at Trelleck and Grosmont, a rarity in South Wales.

Dating of architectural features in Wales can be problematical where few records have survived and where new ideas were sometimes slow to be adopted, and then retained decades after they fell out of fashion in England. Several churches have a window or two which are perhaps late 14th century insertions, and a larger number have features likely to indicate some remodelling in the period 1400 to c1470. The remodelling was fairly thorough at St John's at Cardiff, and in a few other churches. The panelling sometimes found on wall surfaces and the vertical emphasis of window tracery of the period 1360 to 1540 have led to the style being called Perpendicular. New foundations of this era are rare and generally only occurred when an older site nearby was threatened by natural elements.

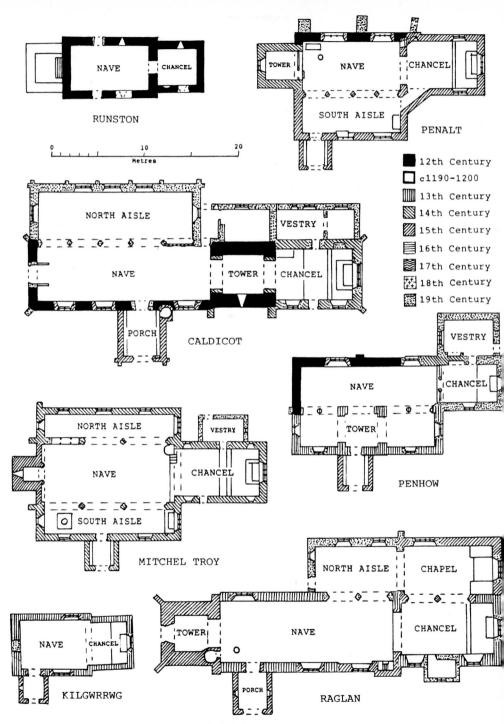

RUNSTON

PENALT

■ 12th Century
□ c1190-1200
13th Century
14th Century
15th Century
16th Century
17th Century
18th Century
19th Century

0   10   20
Metres

CALDICOT

NORTH AISLE

NAVE

TOWER

CHANCEL

VESTRY

PORCH

PENHOW

NAVE

TOWER

CHANCEL

VESTRY

MITCHEL TROY

NORTH AISLE

NAVE

SOUTH AISLE

CHANCEL

VESTRY

KILGWRRWG

NAVE

CHANCEL

RAGLAN

TOWER

NAVE

NORTH AISLE

CHAPEL

CHANCEL

PORCH

PLANS OF GWENT CHURCHES

6

Ewenny

Llysworney

St Hilary

Newcastle Bridgend

TOWERS IN THE VALE OF GLAMORGAN

7

The period c1470 to c1540 was another boom period for building work in Welsh churches although nearly all the work was remodelling of, or additions to, older structures. About half of the medieval church towers of Gwent and Glamorgan are of this period and include the fine structures at St John's at Cardiff. and at the marshland churches of Peterstone and St Bride's Wentloog. All these exibit the blank panelled parapets and corner pinnacles common on towers in adjacent parts of England but rare in Wales. Other notable work includes the Llanquian aisle at Cowbridge, the huge towers at St Bride's Major and Llantrythyd, and aisles at Magor and Penalt.

By 1540 many, but not all, of the bare and dimly lit 12th and 13th century church interiors had been transformed. The large new windows admitted more light although some of them were filled with stained glass (now rarely surviving except in fragments) depicting biblical scenes, lives of saints, or heraldic shields of benefactors. Floors remained rammed earth covered once a year with fresh rushes until the 19th century but there were often now benches for seating the congretation, a pulpit to allow the more recently fashionable preaching of sermons, screens closing off chapels with secondary altars and other fûrnishings such as chests in which plate could be locked. The development of choirs had led to the enlarging of some chancels and the larger churches sometimes retain parts of their stalls. Much woodwork and|stonework was painted and combined with murals and painted coved ceilings with gilded bosses to produce a riot of colour. Unfortunately much of this painting survives today only in a fragmentary faded state. Much must lie hidden under coats of plain whitewash applied in later centuries. Medieval **pulpits** rarely survive but there are fine screens dividing off the chancels at Bettws Newydd, Kemys Commander, Llangwm Uchaf, Redwiok, Trostrey, and Usk Priory, all in Gwent. Some of these supported a rood loft so called from the crucifixion or Rood fixed upon it. These lofts were used as a stage for religious plays and musicians. Organs were then unknown in village churches. Plays were of importance in the conveyance of God's word to the congregation before sermons came fashionable and services were in English or Welsh rather than Latin.

Pyle Church

Skenfrith Church

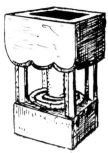

Font at Redwick

Pulpit at Pennard

*St Donats:
Preaching
Cross in
Graveyard*

Little work was carried out upon the fabric of parish churches in Wales during the period 1550 to 1800 beyond minor maintenance, the insertion of a few windows, and the occasional rebuilding or addition of a tower, porch, or chapel as at Chepstow and Llanmaes. The rounded arch reappears in the 16th century and the cusping of the heads of window lights normal in the 14th and 15th centuries drops out of fashion. Large round headed windows became normal in the late 17th and 18th centuries and the pointed arch along with the Gothic style in general was only reintroduced in the middle of the 19th century when there was another building boom with many new churches erected and most of the old ones drastically restored or entirely rebuilt, often with a casting out of most of the medieval furnishings and monuments. The buildings had already been stripped of images and other features which displeased the reformed church.

Carved fragments from screens and lofts removed in this period sometimes found their way into new fittings such as pulpits, stalls, benches, chests, communion rails, and reredoses. Pulpits, sometimes dated, of c1620-40 are fairly common. Some bear classical motifs, and some have a sounding board above. Later three-decker pulpits with lower stalls for lay readers came into fashion. Few survive, but 17th and 18th century woodwork generally is fairly abundant, particularly the communion tables which replaced old altar slabs.

Tomb Chest in Abergavenny Priory Church

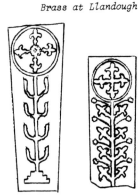

Brass at Llandough

Incised Slab, Christchurch

Grave slabs at Llantwit Major

MONUMENTS

The commonest type of medieval funerary monument in Wales is the coffin lid upon which is incised a floriated cross and sometimes an inscription and/or other motifs. Examples from the 13th century to the 17th can be seen in varying degrees of preservation in several churches. Early grave slabs and cross fragments were sometimes used as sills and lintels for late medieval and post-reformation windows. Fully three dimensional effigies set either in a niche or upon a tomb chest were less common. The two early 13th century knights at Ewenny are the earliest of the thirty or so that survive. Some of them are too damaged for accurate dating and few have remained in situ. Llantwit Major, St Hilary, St Athan, and Llanfihangel Rogiet each have two or three monuments and there are eight at Abergavenny Priory. The tomb at St Bride's Major and the brasses depicting 15th century figures at Llandough and Swansea should also be mentioned.

10

Effigies of the Post-Reformation period are less common, and tomb chests sometimes occur without effigies. There are three tomb chests at Margam, and three damaged effigies at Raglan. Skenfrith has an incised slab upon a tomb chest lacking the pitch normally filling the engraved lines, while Llanvetherine has a shallow relief effigy, and there are rectangular brass plates with figures at Llangattock and Llanover. These are poor in quality compared with the medieval cut out figures which are more deeply engraved. Goldcliff has a brass plate recording the tidal flooding of the coastal marshlands in 1606, and plain brass inscriptions occur elsewhere. A 16th century development was the wall-monument with a person or couple kneeling, or as demi-figures, the effigies being sometimes quite small. A 17th century example can be seen at Cowbridge. After the Civil War effigies of any kind were unusual and tablets became the norm. However these can be quite elaborate with not only inscriptions but heraldry, putti, symbols of death or trade or status or claim to fame.

Tomb Slab at Llanvetherine

Carne Monument at Cowbridge

HERE LYETH THE BODIES OF WILLM PRICHARD OF LANOVOR ESQVIRE · &C OF MATHEW PRICHARD OF LANOVOR ESQ. HIS SONNE AND HEIRE LINEALLY DESCENDED FROM THE BODYE OF CRADOCKE VRAICHVRAS EARLE OF HEREFORD & PRINCE BETWEENE WYE AND SEAVERNE

Early 17th century brass at Llanover

Tower of St John's Church, Abergavenny   *William Baker's tomb, Abergavenny Priory*

GAZETTEER OF CHURCHES IN GWENT

ABERGAVENNY *St John*   SO 300142

In the middle of the town stands the embattled tower of the former
parish church of St John. When the priory church was taken over by
the townsfolk in the 1540s St John's became the chapel of Henry
VIII's new grammar school. The unaisled nave also partly survives.

ABERGAVENNY *St Mary*   SO 301141

This large cruciform church served a priory founded by Hamelin de
Ballon in c1100. When dissolved in 1536 there were only a prior and
four monks. The nave was already used by the townsfolk, who then
took over the whole building. For a while the chancel was used as
a school but is now part of the church again. It and the transepts
are essentially 14th century work, altered after being ravaged by
Owain Glyndwr in 1402, and since several times restored. The nave and
north aisle were entirely rebuilt in 1882-96. Among the furnishings
are a Norman font, probably from another church, late medieval choir
stalls with miserichords carved with various motifs, and a wooden
representation of the tree of Jesse, probably from a reredos. On a
board in the south transept are Royal Arms dating from 1709.

There are more effigies in Abergavenny Priory than any other
Welsh church. The oak effigy of a knight, although labelled George
de Cantilupe, d1273, is more likely to be a member of the Hastings
family up to a half century later. In the north chapel are a pair
of small females, probably Margaret of Windsor and Joan de Cantilupe,
plus the monument of David Lewis, d1584. In the south chapel are
Lawrence de Hastings, d1348, last resident Lord of Abergavenny,
William de Hastings, d1349, William ap Thomas, d1446, and his wife
Gwladys, Sir Richard Herbert, beheaded 1459, and his wife Margaret,
Richard Herbert, d1510, Judge Andrew Powell, d1635, and William
Baker, d1648, who kneels towards his wife Joan.

BASSALEG *St Basil*   ST 277892

The church lies on a hill above the Ebbw River. The long nave and south aisle have no datable features, all the windows being renewed. Set either side of the south doorway are the headstops of the hood mould of the original doorway. The lofty west tower and chancel are 15th century. The south porch and the vestries are 19th century.

BEDWELTY *St Sannan*   ST 166004

The church lies high above the Rhymney Valley on the border between Gwent and Glamorgan. The 15th century west tower was built prior to the nave and north aisle being thrown into one body by removing the arcade, but the chancel, with a 15th century priest's doorway, was added afterwards. The nave south wall may be 13th century. All the windows, and the porch and vestry, are 19th century. There is a chest with crude carvings of the Passion and floral decorations.

BETTWS *Dedication Unknown*   SO 297193

This single celled 13th century chapel lies in a remote valley to the north of Abergavenny. The triple east lancets are original. On the south side is a blocked 15th century doorway. The west doorway and the south window are 19th century.

BETTWS *Dedication Unknown*   ST 289904

This tiny 13th century nave and chancel church was a chapel-of-ease to Newport until the 17th century. The features are all Victorian.

BETTWS NEWYDD *Dedication Unknown*   SO 362058

The single chamber and west porch are unrestored. The fine screen with a roodloft still retaining an original cross on the panelling, the coved wagon roof, good east window, and other features are all of c1450-1500. There is a Norman font on a later base.

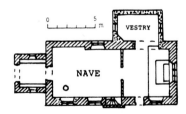

PLAN OF BETTWS NEWYDD CHURCH

Bettws Chapel

Bettws Church

Bryngwyn Church

Caldicot Church

BISHTON *St Cadwaladr* ST 387873

The nave and chancel are probably both 14th century, each having a
window of that date. The nave north doorway and the window by the
chancel NE corner are 15th century, as is the embattled west tower,
crookedly set to the nave, with a polygonal NE stair turret. From
the chancel arch project the heads of a monk, nun, man, and chubby
cheeked woman. The font and stoup are medieval. The north porch is
a 19th century addition.

BRYNGWYN *St Peter* SO 390094

According to Gerald of wales Aeddan Gweathfoed, Lord of Clytha, was
the founder of churches at Bettws Newydd, Clytha, and Bryngwyn in
the mid 12th century. So some of the nave masonry at Bryngwyn may
be that early. The west doorway is 13th century. Not much later a
tiny tower was added against it. One nave south window, the timber
south porch, and the chancel with one original SW window, are 14th
century. Other windows in the nave and chancel, and the rood stair,
are 15th century. The chancel arch and the north aisle with a two
bay arcade are 19th century. The hexagonal font is probably 14th
century, and there is an old iron bound chest plus a memorial stone
to William Tyler, who died in 1695.

CAERLEON *St Cadoc* ST 339906

The church lies in a spacious close in the middle of the town. It
lies upon the site of the headquarters building of the Roman fort.
It has an aisled nave, a chancel and south chapel, a small but high
SW tower, a south porch, and large NE vestries. The tower contains
a Norman arch but is essentially 13th century with a 15th century
embattled top. The nave west wall and north aisle outer wall are
also medieval but the rest was rebuilt or added in the 1860s and
1930s. The chancel windows have glass commemorating Charles Williams,
d1720, a benefactor of the church. He fled abroad after killing his
cousin in a duel on Penrhos Hill but returned to a pardon after
making a fortune as a trader in Smyrna.

14

CAERWENT *St Stephen* ST 468905

The long 13th century chancel has renewed lancets to the east and north, and Victorian vestries to the south. The west tower, with a polygonal SE stair turret, and the ashlar faced nave north wall, with two fine windows and a porch with fleurons on the outer arch, are all 15th century. The south aisle is rebuilt except for the 13th century arcade of plain pointed arches on square pillars. In the aisle are two 13th century floriated cross slabs and two fonts, one of which came from a former church at Dinham. The pulpit bears the year 1632, carvings of flowers, foliage, and Llandaff Cathedral, and an inscription 'Woe until me if I preach not the Gospel'. The cherub on the chancel wall commemorates four 18th century babies who each in turn 'Just peeped and uttered infant cries, Disliked the scene, and shut their eyes'.

CALDICOT *St Mary* ST 484886

The Norman central tower retains one original round headed window on the south side. The much restored chancel and the buttresses of the tower are 14th century, and the long nave, large south porch, and the embattled tower top are 15th century. The porch entrance has a fine ogival arch with pinnacles. The north aisle and arcade and the nave windows and doorways are of the mid 19th century.

CATS ASH *St Curig* ST 372907

A 14th century chapel is incorporated in the buildings of a house of 1604. The blocked east window can be seen from the roadside. The north wall has gone and the divided interior is now storage space.

Caerleon Church

Caerwent Church

Chepstow Priory Church

Tower at Chepstow

CHEPSTOW *St Mary*   ST 536940

William Fitz-Osbern founded a Benedictine Priory here in c1070. Of it there remain the early 12th century nave which has blocked plain round arches which formerly gave onto aisles. Above is a gallery with two-light openings, with a low clerestory above. Originally the nave was of six bays and then there was a central tower with transepts and chapels flanking a chancel. However the tower fell in c1700 destroying the east end of the church. A new tower with such classical features as windows with triangular pediments was raised within the western bay of the nave in 1706. A new chancel and two transeptal chapels were not erected until 1891. The arcade pier of the north chapel stands upon the massive base of the original pier supporting the NW corner of the former tower. There are fonts from the 12th and 15th centuries, the 16th century tomb and effigies of Henry, 2nd Earl of Worcester and his wife Elizabeth Brown, the 17th century monument of Margaret Cleyton and her husbands Thomas and Richard, and a 17th century organ formerly in Gloucester Cathedral, brought to Chepstow from Bristol Cathedral in 1685.

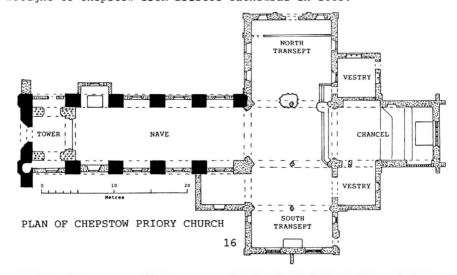

PLAN OF CHEPSTOW PRIORY CHURCH

16

Christchurch Church   *Cwmcarvan Church*

CHRISTCHURCH *Holy Trinity*   SO 347894

The large church was heavily restored in the 19th century and again
in 1955 after an arson attack in 1949. So the arcade piers are new,
the late medieval ones being very different, with complex mouldings.
The re-set south doorway with chevrons is Norman and the chancel
is 13th century, original features being the piscina, north lancet,
and the stumps of three east lancets visible outside. The aisle
outer walls, south porch, and the high tower west of the south aisle
are 15th century. The tower originally had an embattled parapet.
In the chancel is an incised slab with figures of John and Isabella
Colmer, d1376, with a floriated cross between them. The stone was
long considered to have miraculous powers of healing on the Eve
of Ascension Day. As late as 1770 sixteen children were laid upon it
all night in the hope of being cured by the morning.

CRICK *St Nyven*   ST 490903

A small early 14th century manorial single cell chapel became a barn
in the 18th century, and has recently been converted into a house.

CWMCARVAN *St Clement*   SO 477075

The interesting church lies almost alone. East of the porch is the
blocked original Norman doorway. In the 15th century the nave was
lengthened and provided with a north porch (now a vestry), fine new
windows, and a roodloft stair. The south porch and the ashlar faced
west tower were added in c1500. The chancel was rebuilt in the 16th
century. The tower has a NE stair turret, two light belfry windows
with the tracery above the main lights left unpierced, and a heavy
moulding following the contour of the battlements. In the tower are
an iron studded door and a black oak screen of c1600. The roof is
painted dark blue with gold bosses. There are an old font and two
13th century floriated cross slabs, plus an altar table of 1637.

17

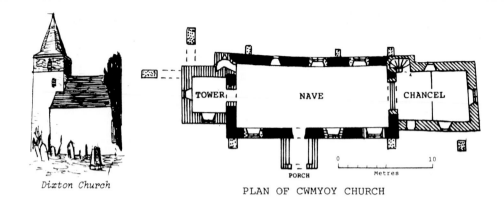

Dixton Church

PLAN OF CWMYOY CHURCH

CWMYOY *St Martin*   SO 299233

The church lies on a shelf above the Honddu so affected by landslips
that the walls now lean at a variety of crazy angles. Even with the
support of huge flying buttresses it is difficult to see how the
west tower remains standing. The south doorway with a roll moulded
segmental head, the font, and perhaps one north window are Norman.
Two south windows are late 13th and 16th century respectively and
three others are Victorian. The chancel has an east window of c1330
but the south lancet and priest's doorway may be earlier. The 13th
or 14th century porch contains a stoup re-set on the wall.

DINGESTOW *St Dingat*   SO 457104

The dedication is unique. The nave has two 15th century windows in
the south wall. The church has been otherwise mostly rebuilt.

Cwmyoy Church

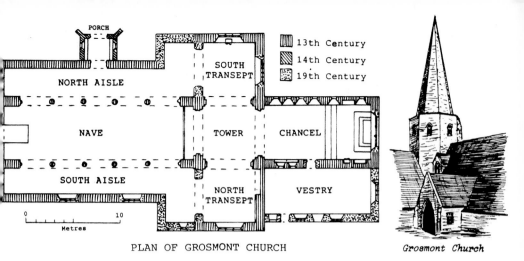

PLAN OF GROSMONT CHURCH

Grosmont Church

Legend:
- 13th Century
- 14th Century
- 19th Century

DIXTON *St Peter*   SO 520136

The church lies by the Wye, shielded from the busy A40 by trees.
The long nave has herringbone masonry concealed beneath whitewash.
The windows and vestries are 19th century. The chancel has a 15th
century north window. The priest's doorway may be earlier. Of the
14th century are the tiny west tower with cusped lancets in the
belfry stage and a dumpy broach spire, and the north porch with a
re-set medieval sculpture of St Peter being nailed to a cross.

GOLDCLIFF *Dedication Unknown*   ST 365832

The main body of the church is 12th century, the short tower is
14th century, and the porch is medieval, but there are no features
of interest, the openings all being renewed. Over the porch outer
entrance is a sundial dated 1729. In the chancel is a brass plate
commemorating that "On the 20th day of January, 1606, even as it
came to pass, it pleased God the flud (tide) did flow to the edge
of this same bras, and in this parish there was lost £5000 in
stock etc, besides 22 people drowned."

GOYTREY *Dedication Unknown*

The church lies among yews. It was rebuilt in 1846 but contains a
Norman font with cable moulding and semi-circles, and an old chest.

GROSMONT *St Nicholas*   SO 405243

This is a large cruciform church mostly of c1220-1300. The chancel
is the earliest part and the only part now in use for services. It
has seven renewed lancets in the north wall and a large Victorian
vestry on the south side. The transepts have end windows indicating
a date close to c1300. Their western bays are Victorian. The south
transept contains a Norman font decorated with cable moulding and
roundels, a large but crude (perhaps unfinished) effigy of a knight,
and a slab with a light relief depicting Henry Gabb, d1708. The
aisled nave with five bay arcades is of c1270-1300. Of the 14th
century are the double piscina in the chancel, the octagonal upper
stage of the tower with a spire, the north porch, and the window
with reticulated tracery in the nave west wall.

19

GWERNESNEY *St Michael* SO 415017

Both the nave and chancel and the arch between them are of the 13th century. The heads on the west doorway hoodmould may be older work re-set. Above is an original lancet, and there are cusped lancets in the north and east walls. The porch and two south windows are 15th century, and west of the porch is a 16th century window. There is an old screen in the chancel arch.

HENLLYS *Dedication Unknown* ST 267911

The church lies far south of the village with just one farm beside it. The nave and chancel with the chancel arch and south doorway are 13th century. Of the 15th century are the chancel windows and priest's doorway and the west tower with a plain parapet and a tiny embattled NE stair turret. The large south porch is probably 16th century, and the window west of it is perhaps of the 17th century.

ITTON *St Deiniol* ST 494953

The nave and chancel have 13th century masonry but the windows and south doorway are Victorian. The original pointed chancel arch is flanked on either side by smaller modern arches filled with iron grilles. On the arch are heads of a curly headed man and a humourous faced woman in a draped cap. The tower of c1300 has traces of the former west doorway below a window with Y-tracery. The rubble top parts are a repair after a lightning strike in the 18th century. Inside are an old font and memorials to the Curres of Itton Court.

KEMYS COMMANDER *All Saints* SO 349048

The hexagonal font may be 14th century but the whole of the small church, which was originally dedicated to St John the Baptist, is 15th century. The west and south doorways, timber west porch, the windows, the coved wagon roof with floral bosses and moulded ribs, and the dark oak screen are all original. A narrow south window once lighted the former roodloft above the screen.

KEMYS INFERIOR *All Saints* ST 381928

Only foundations hidden in woods between the A449 and the Wye now remain of this church, which had a Norman west doorway and later medieval windows. It was demolished in 1960-2, being dangerous.

KILGWRRWG *Holy Cross* SO 463985

This remote church has to be approached on foot across fields from a solitary farm at the end of a lane. The blocked west doorway and most of the walling is 13th century. The side windows of the nave are 16th century. The south doorway and porch are probably slightly earlier. The double bellcote at the west end is of uncertain date. The nave roof has original tie-beams and queen posts.

LANGSTONE *Dedication Unknown* ST 372892

The western third of the nave was probably added in 1622, the date on the west doorway. Otherwise the church is mostly 13th century. One original lancet, perhaps re-set from the original west wall, is in the north wall. The south doorway and a north window are 15th century, and the vestry and organ recess are 19th century.

Llanbadoc Church

LLANARTH *St Teilo* SO 375109

The long nave and narrow chancel both have 13th century doorways and the chancel also retains two lancets. The porch is 14th century and of the 15th century are the ashlar faced tower with pinnacles, two south windows, and the rood staircase also giving access to the pulpit.   There is also an old chest.

LLANBADOC *St Madoc* SO 376001

The church lies below a lane beside the Usk south of Usk town. The slender west tower with an embattled parapet upon a corbel table and plain rectangular belfry windows may be late 13th century. The long nave with its south doorway, and the chancel with one southern lancet are certainly of that era. The priest's doorway, two south windows, and the porch with an ogival headed hoodmould over the outer entrance are 15th century, and the three bay north aisle and vestry were added during a heavy restoration in 1877.

LLANDDEWI FACH *St David* SO 332958

The mostly rebuilt, and now disused, church lies at the end of a lane. The round arched west doorway is 16th century and the walling of the nave and chancel may partly go back to the 13th century.

LLANDDEWI RHYDDERCH *St David* SO 349129

The chancel east window with three cusped lights is of c1300. That dates the nave and chancel walling, although the other features are 19th century. The Norman west tower has tiny original windows on either side, a tower arch of c1300, and a later recessed timber top.

LLANDDEWI SKIRRID *St David* SO 341170

The church was rebuilt in 1879 except for the 14th century tower. Traces of a chapel of St Michael lie on the summit of Skirrid Fawr.

LLANDEGFEDD *St Tegfedd* SO 338958

The nave may be as early as c1100. It has a small north window and
a round arched west doorway. The chancel is also Norman, but later.
It retains one original window and the priest's doorway. One nave
window is contemporary. There is a 14th century south window and
there is old woodwork in the west porch and coved roof. The church
was heavily restored in the 19th century and the blocked NW doorway
led to a vestry added then but subsequently demolished.

LLANDENNY *St John* SO 303109

The position of the Norman south doorway suggests the nave was later
lengthened westwards. There is also one Norman window. The chancel
is late 13th century and has an old roof and a plain original altar
stone. The porch and the west tower with a NE stair turret are 15th
century. The octagonal font is dated 1661.

LLANDERFEL *St Derfel* ST 264953

Slight traces of an L-shaped building lie west of a farm beside a
track from Upper Cwmbran to Henllys. Derfel Gadarn, veteran of the
battle of Camlan in which King Arthur died, supposedly retired here.

LLANELLEN *St Helen* SO 304109

In a thorough Victorian restoration the chancel was rebuilt and the
nave lengthened and given a spired turret. The nave and chancel arch
are 13th century, and three windows, the south doorway and porch,
and the coved roof of the nave and porch are 15th century. In the
chancel are two high backed chairs of c1700.

LLANELLY *St Elli* ST 233148

This church lay in Breconshire until 1974. The south walls of the
nave and chancel are 13th century. In c1500 the chancel was widened
and given a north chapel with a two bay arcade, whilst the nave was
given an aisle with a three bay arcade, since renewed, and a large
tower was added with a SW stair turret. The aisle and chapel are
undivided. The south porch is 13th or 14th century.

LLANFIHANGEL CRUCORNEY *St Michael* SO 325206

The long nave, most of which is now roofless, and the chancel with
two lancet windows, a two light window, and the priest's doorway
are 13th century. The original west doorway now opens into a lofty
embattled west tower added, along with the south porch, in the 15th
century. There is a monument to Richard Scudamore, d1667.

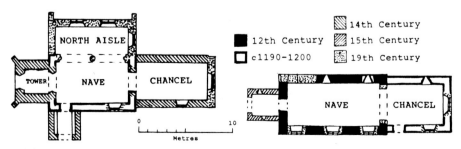

PLAN OF LLANFIHANGEL NEAR ROGIETT CHURCH   PLAN OF LLANDEGFEDD CHURCH

Llanfihangel Crucorney Church

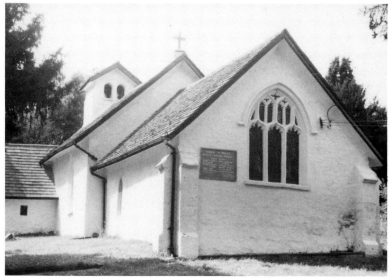

Llanfihangel Pontymoel Church

LLANFIHANGEL NEAR ROGIET *St Michael*   ST 452878

The Late Norman nave has a round arched doorway by the SW corner. The tower, south porch, and chancel with one cusped window are 14th century, the tower battlements are 16th century, one plain south window is of c1600, and the chancel east wall and the north aisle with a two bay arcade are 19th century. The chancel arch has heads of women with coils of hair around their ears. The font may be 12th century. There is a tomb with an effigy of Anne Martel, d1270, with a greyhound at her feet, while the damaged effigy of a cross-legged knight in the chancel may be her husband John.

LLANFIHANGEL NIGH USK *St Michael*   SO 347092

The NE and SW corners of the nave are probably Norman. The chancel, the narrow north aisle with three posts rising to a horizontal beam instead of an arcade, the rood stair and adjacent window, and the tower belfry windows are 15th century. The tower itself, which has a low pyramidal roof, may be earlier. One north window has carvings of a heart and shears in the spandrel, and another has intertwined hearts. The south porch is mostly rebuilt but has one original side window. The octagonal font has a heart on each side of the base and interlaced hearts around the bowl. At the SW corner is a carving showing angels guiding a soul up to heaven.

LLANFIHANGEL PONTYMOEL *St Michael*   SO 302012

The cream-washed walls and 19th century windows make the church look fairly recent, but the nave and chancel are both medieval and the thick west wall supporting a bellcote has an old doorway. The porch is dated 1736 and there are an old chest and font.

LLANFIHANGEL TOR-Y-MYNYDD *St Michael*   SO 465018

The nave, chancel, and porch are all of c1470-1520. The doorways, three south windows, double bellcote and chancel arch are original. Only the north and west windows are Victorian.

23

Llangattock Lingoed Church

LLANFOIST *St Helen* SO 287132

The church is hidden away behind the village, south of Abergavenny. The round arched priest's doorway, although renewed, is of c1200, and the nave masonry may be Late Norman. The chancel windows are Victorian but the nave windows and south doorway are late medieval and the west doorway may be 14th century.

LLANGATTOCK LINGOED *St Cadoc* SO 362200

From the north the church appears long and low. The two light belfry windows look 14th century but the tower battlements upon moulded corbel coursing, are late 15th century. The NE stair turret rises slightly higher. Several windows, the doorways, south porch, and the beam carved with grapes and vine leaves set in front of the chancel arch which is all that remains of the screen, are all 15th century. The east window has cusped lights set above and below a transom. Inside are coved roofs and a Norman font.

LLANGATTOCK NIGH USK *St Cadoc* SO 330097

The nave and chancel form a single body with several 15th century windows. The nave roof was made flush with that of the chancel in 1827. The nave and tower masonry may be 13th century. The latter has a pyramidal roof. The rood stair projection, and perhaps the porch, are 15th century. On the chancel south wall is a brass with a figure of Zirophaeniza Mathewe, wife of Andrew Powell, d1625, and in the nave floor is a floriated cross slab dated 1653.

LLANGATTOCK VIBON AVEL *St Cadoc* SO 457157

Only the 14th century porch tower on the south side is medieval. The rest dates from 1875. The church lies hidden below a house.

LLANGEVIEW *Dedication Unknown*

This lonely church has a small nave likely to be Norman. One south window and the chancel are 16th century. Also old are the west porch and belfry. There are oak seats in the chancel.

LLANGOVAN *St Govan* SO 456055

The narrow nave and chancel both date from c1200, having a round chancel arch, two small lancets near the nave east end, and a third in the chancel north wall. Two other chancel windows, and possibly the nave south doorway, are 14th century, whilst the west doorway and two windows are 15th century. The porch is old but is much restored. The small stone belfry raised upon a pair of piers inside is not old. The chancel floor is entirely paved with 17th century tombstones.

LLANGUA SO 390257

The church lies alone beside the A465. The south doorway appears Norman externally but the rere-arch looks 14th century. There is a pretty timber framed 17th century bell turret at the west end. The wider chancel having thin walls is probably of the 16th century, the period of the uncusped three light east window.

HIC IACET ZIROPHÆNIZA FILIA WILL-
HELMI MATHEWE DE RADYR IN COMITA
GLAMORGAN ARMIG NVPER VXOR AN-
DREÆ POWELL ARMIG QVÆ OBIJT DECI
OCTAVO DIE MENSIS FEBRVARII ANNO
VICESSIMO SECVNDO IACOBI REGIS

Brass at Llangattock-Nigh-Usk Church

Llangovan Church

LLANGWM ISAF *St John* SO 429006

Two churches only a kilometre apart at Llangwm Isaf and Llangwm Uchaf formerly served separate parishes. One passes St John's first. The single chamber was rebuilt from the foundations in the 19th century and a chancel arch then inserted. Two 15th century windows have been re-set. There is a west porch.

LLANGWM UCHAF *St Jerome* SO 434006

St Jerome's is the larger and most interesting of the two churches. Both nave and chancel are 13th century, with several cusped lancets, and two light windows with circles over the lights in the east and west walls. The south doorway is original but the porch and a south window are 15th century. Of c1480-1520 are the tower on the north side of the chancel and the rood screen which is the glory of the church. The tower stair in a polygonal turret gives onto the loft.

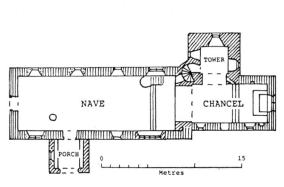

PLAN OF LLANGWM UCHAF CHURCH

Llangwm Uchaf Church

LLANGYBI *St Cybi* ST 374967

The church has a west tower, a blocked SW doorway, and several fine windows of the 15th century. The double roodloft staircases, one on each side, are very unusual. The nave is the same width as the chancel and may have older masonry. Inside are a font of 1662 with coats of arms and flower medallions, an oak communion table dated 1632, and a Georgian pulpit with a square sounding board.

LLANHENNOCK *St John* ST 354927

The nave has a 14th or 15th century SW doorway and the chancel has a blocked 16th century priest's doorway. Both nave and chancel may be of 13th century origin but were much restored in the 19th century when a porch and two bay north aisle were added. The embattled west tower with a NE stair turret is 15th century.

Llanhennock Church

LLANHILLETH *St Illtyd*   ST 218020

The church lies 350m up south of Abertillery. The nave may be 12th or 13th century but lacks ancient features. The saddleback roofed tower is perhaps 13th century, and the chancel is 15th century. The latter inclines to the north.

LLANLLOWELL *St Llywel*   ST 393986

The small single chamber is Norman, with an original west window, and a south doorway with a large lintel. Also Norman is the font. The north lancet and two light east window are 13th century and the roodloft staircase and the adjacent priest's doorway and window are 15th century. The porch is old but without datable features.

LLANMARTIN *St Martin*   ST 395894

Only the embattled 15th century tower with a NE stair turret has survived a 19th century rebuilding. The recessed altar tomb in the chancel is probably that of Sir Thomas Morgan of Pencoed Castle, d1510. The recess has headstops of a man with a moustache and a gryphon supporting a castle. Also in the chancel are three chairs, two with surmounting eagles, dating from the 17th century.

Llanover Church

LLANOVER *St Bartholomew* SO 318094

The rendered nave walls have a doorway with sunk quadrant mouldings indicating a date of c1300, but the windows are 19th century. The partly refaced chancel has a 15th century east window. Of the late 15th century is the fine ashlar faced three stage tower with a NE stair turret. The porch is dated 1750 and the altar rails are dated 1700. The Norman font has a cable moulding and daisies and wheels. Let into the side of one of two late 16th century oak box pews is a brass of 1610 depicting William and Matthew Pritchard in armour with folded arms and pointed beards. Another inscription recalls Walter Ramsey, made a judge in 1631, dismissed by Parliament in 1647, and reinstated at the Restoration just before his death.

LLANSOY *St Tysoi* SO 442023

Most of the features of the west tower, nave, chancel, and south porch are 15th or 16th century, but the nave masonry and the west doorway now opening into the tower may be 13th or 14th century. The best of the late medieval features is the moulded porch outer entrance. There are coved roofs. In the vestry is an old chest.

LLANSSANTFRAED *St Bridget* SO 009357

There is a Norman font and the small nave and chancel may have some Norman walling, although most of the windows are Victorian. The two small alabaster reliefs of the burial and resurrection of Christ in the wall by the altar probably formed part of an altarpiece. In the chancel is an inscription to Sir Christopher Hatton, d1624.

Llanssantfraed Church

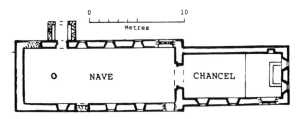

PLAN OF LLANTHONY CHURCH

LLANTARNAM *St Michael*   ST 307912

The nave, chancel arch, and south doorway are probably 14th century. The embattled west tower with a NE stair turret was added in the 15th century when the chancel was rebuilt. The wide north chapel is late 16th century. The two curious arches opening to it from the chancel may be slightly earlier work salvaged from Llantarnam Abbey. Three nave windows are also 16th century. The vestry and porch are 19th century. There are numerous 18th century memorial tablets.

LLANTHONY *St David*   SO 288279

The church lies immediately south of the ruined abbey and the nave is formed out of the infirmary hall, whilst the chancel was once a chapel opening out of the east wall. The result is what appears to be the least altered nave and chancel church of c1190-1210 in South Wales, the chancel arch and several windows being original. A north porch was added during the restoration of 1897.

Llanthony Church

Llantilio Crosseny Church

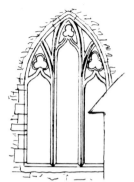

Window, Llantilio Crosseny

Machen Church

LLANTILIO CROSSENY *St Teilo*

SO 399149

Patronage by the lords of White Castle has resulted in a larger and more interesting church than is usual for a small Gwent village. The central tower upon four narrow pointed arches is early 13th century. The much wider chancel of c1300 east of it has several good windows, plus a slightly later one. Instead of true transepts there are chapels flanking both the tower and part of the chancel, that on the north being by far the larger. Both are 14th century but incorporate the remains of proper 13th century transepts. The comparatively narrow 14th century nave has aisles with fine four bay arcades, and a spacious west porch. The aisle outer windows are Victorian. Under the crossing can be seen four timbers which support the framework for the bells. The broach spire is probably 14th century in origin but was rebuilt in 1709. The doorway over the west crossing arch gave access to the former rood loft. There is a Norman font. The Cil Llwych chapel has a squint pointing to the high altar, Jacobean altar rails, and corbel image brackets either side of the east window with carvings of young men with circlets around their curly hair. Hidden under the choir stalls is a stone to Owen Rogers, a vicar ejected by the Puritans, and there are two others, one being to a man who died in 1621 and who is shown bearded in a ruff and a long coat. His wife has a ruff and a veil.

30

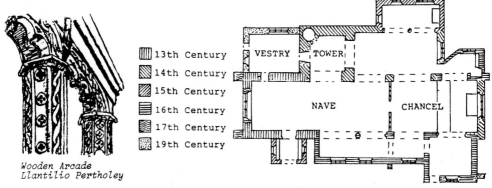

13th Century
14th Century
15th Century
16th Century
17th Century
19th Century

Wooden Arcade
Llantilio Pertholey

PLAN OF LLANTILIO PERTHOLEY CHURCH

VESTRY TOWER

NAVE CHANCEL

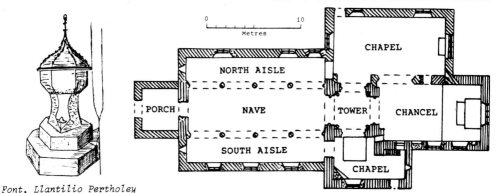

0   10
Metres

Font, Llantilio Pertholey

CHAPEL

NORTH AISLE

PORCH NAVE TOWER CHANCEL

SOUTH AISLE

CHAPEL

PLAN OF LLANTILIO CROSSENY CHURCH

LLANTILIO PERTHOLEY *St Teilo* SO 312163

Some 13th century masonry may remain in the nave, but the oldest
datable part is the north tower with a shouldered lintelled 14th
century doorway to the staircase. The east and south arches must be
contemporary with the north chapel of c1350-1400. An extra bay was
added to the chancel and the south porch built in the 15th century.
At the end of the medieval period chapels were added north of the
chancel east end and the north chapel, the latter having a timber
two bay arcade. The south chapel is 16th century and the NW vestry
is 20th century. The nave west window is of 1729. The church was
damaged by fire in 1974 but an almsbox dated 1704, an old chest, and
the octagonal font with fleur-de-lys on the base luckily survived.

LLANTRISSANT *St Bartholomew* ST 393948

This chapel-of-ease became a cowshed in the 18th century but fell
down earlier this century. The minimal remains lie in a field.

LLANTRISSANT *SS Peter, Paul, & John* ST 391969

The wide nave and the much narrower chancel each have 13th century
doorways, and the chancel has a cusped lancet. One north window and
the west tower are 15th century, and the porch and a south window
are 16th century. Other windows are Victorian. Over the porch outer
arch is a sundial dated 1718. In the chancel are two 17th century
chairs and a Jacobean oak altar table. The font is dated 1673.

LLANVACHES *St Dubritius* ST 434916

The church has been much restored. The blocked round arched north
doorway is of c1200. The south doorway and porch are late medieval.
The saddleback roofed tower may be 13th century although the arch
to the nave is 14th century while the SE stair turret has a 15th
century doorway. The octagonal font is 14th century. Framed in the
tower is the will of William Wroth, rector here from 1611 to 1639,
when he was expelled for refusing to read Laud's declaration about
Sunday sports. He founded the first Welsh non-conformist chapel.

LLANVAIR DISCOED *St Mary* ST 447924

The small nave and chancel may be 15th century. The segmental arched
south doorway is original but the windows are all Victorian. There
are several 18th century monuments fixed upon the chancel walls.

LLANVAIR KILGEDDIN *St Mary* SO 356087

The church lies within a wide bend of the River Usk far from the
village it served and is now disused. The round arched nave doorway
may be 16th century, and there are two late medieval north windows.
The west and south walls are rebuilt. The chancel has a late 13th
century north window and a priest's doorway and window of the 15th
century. The font and 15th century screen were imported in 1876.

LLANVAPLEY *St Mabli* SO 366141

The Norman nave walls have a pronounced external batter. The west
tower of c1300 has Y-tracery in the west window. The south doorway
and the chancel with twin east lancets and a cinquefoiled circle
are late 13th century. The chancel has a coved roof and contains
old altar railing. There is a stone to Peter Powell, d1626, and a
monument with flying angels and strange beasts to the barrister
William Parry, who died in 1703.

Llanvapley Church

Llanwenarth Church

Llanvetherine Church

LLANVETHERINE *St Veterinus*   SO 364172

Traces of the original 12th or 13th century south doorway appear above the present 15th century doorway. Two south windows are also 15th century, and the window which once lighted a roodloft is dated 1703 over the round head, whilst the plain north windows are 16th or 17th century. The chancel added in c1330 has a fine east window with three cusped lancets. The ogival headed window is 14th century and the roodloft stair is 15th century. The 16th century tower has the belfry stage projected out on a corbel table. On the chancel floor is a cross slab dated 1601 and on the east wall are a pair of light reliefs. One is to David Powell, who died in 1621 after 43 years as rector. The other shows a woman with a Welsh hat and the date 1715. The 15th century porch has a broken off holy water stoup and a figure of St Veterinus in priestly robes with a book in his left hand and his right hand raised in a blessing.

LLANVIHANGEL YSTERN LLEWERN *St Michael*   SO 433138

Both the late 13th century nave and chancel retain several original windows and doorways, the chancel doorway being unusually lofty. One south window is 15th century. The font is Norman. On the north wall is an elaborate but rustic relief in memory of a rector's son William Hopkins, d1698. A blue eyed, rosy cheeked, angel with golden hair supports the inscription. Three pistols are on the coat of arms above. Monsters with bird-like heads writhe round the sides, and chained to them are a pair of stags nibbling at branches of foliage. Above all are two more figures, a woman and an angel with a horn. The timber belfry is supported on a beam at the west end.

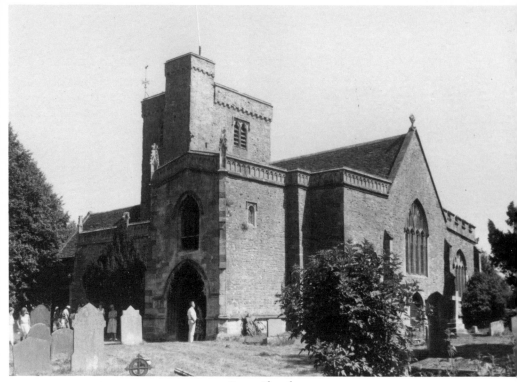

Magor Church

LLANWENARTH *St Peter*   SO 276148

One north window and the south doorway date the long chancel and
nave to c1300. The ogival headed priest's doorway, three chancel
windows with reticulated tracery, and one nave window are of c1330.
The blocked nave west window may be a relic of an older church. A
tower was built against it in the 14th or 15th century. The porch
is still later. In the church is a Norman font.

LLANWERN *St Mary*   ST 371879

The small 15th century single bodied church with a south porch and
diagonally buttressed west tower lies above the huge steelworks.
The windows have fragments of medieval Flemish stained glass.

MACHEN *St Michael*   ST 228881

The 13th century tower arch and chancel arch are simply pointed,
and probably the tower, wide nave, and wide but short chancel are
all of that date, although the windows are mostly Victorian. The
tower has a 15th century west doorway and battlements on a corbel
table. The south porch and north chapel are 16th century. On the
nave walls are the arms of several of the Morgans of Plas Machen,
and there are several 18th century monuments to them in the chapel.
The largest is to Sir William Morgan, d1725. In the tower is part
of the pediment of a Romano-Celtic shrine. It has a worn carving of
a Gorgon's head with huge staring eyes. The original church here
was founded in the 6th century by Glywys ap Tegid and Ynyr Gwent.

Mamhilad Church

MAGOR *St Mary* ST 425869

St Cadwalader, the last Welsh ruler to consider himself as King of Britain, founded this church in the 7th century. The stones with chevrons re-set on the chancel are relics of a Norman church here dedicated to St Leonard. A new cruciform church with a central tower and transepts was built in the early 13th century. Before long the chancel was rebuilt larger, and in the early 14th century a large new east window was inserted and narrow aisles added to the nave. The panelled font and the splendid porch with a lierne vault and an open trefoiled parapet are 15th century. The porch upper storey was once used as a school room. In c1500 the arcades and transepts were remodelled and the aisles widened except for at the west end of the north aisle where the porch prevented this. There is a worn head of a bishop on the west doorway, and there are faces on the window headstops. The transept arches are panelled. The transepts now house the organ and vestry. The arcades are adorned with twenty eight vigorous figures of angels. On the NW side of the churchyard are ruins of late medieval buildings belonging to a small priory.

MALPAS *Dedication Unknown* ST 308896

Of a modest Norman church which served a small priory only the south doorway and chancel arch survived rebuilding in the 19th century.

MAMHILAD *St Illtyd* SO 305034

The fine east window, the porch, priest's doorway, and three other windows are 15th century but the nave and chancel walls may be 14th century, the probable date of the west porch, chancel arch and SW window. The west gallery contains fragments of a medieval screen with traceried panels and fruit and flowers, and the east window has 18th century glass showing the Crucifixion.

Marshfield Church

MARSHFIELD *St Mary* ST 262826

The chief features of interest are the Norman south doorway with floral patterned capitals on the side shafts, the early 13th century doorway in the otherwise rebuilt west tower, the large 15th century porch with fleurons in the outer arch, and a floriated cross slab set into a wall. The other features are all renewed. The very long nave may have been lengthened before the tower was added.

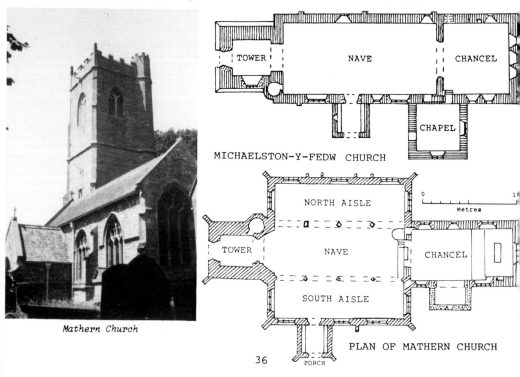

Mathern Church

MICHAELSTON-Y-FEDW CHURCH

PLAN OF MATHERN CHURCH

MATHERN *St Tewdric*

The church and the palace of the Bishops of Llandaff lie together at the end of a lane beyond the village. The three round arches of the north arcade are of c1200. The pointed western arch was added in the 13th century when the loftier four bay south arcade and and chancel were built. The chancel has triple east lancets, a double piscina, and a north lancet. The embattled west tower with diagonal buttresses and a polygonal NE stair turret was added in c1480 by Bishop Marshall, and the aisle outer walls, south porch, and four chancel windows are also 15th century work. Shields on the tower have the initial M and an eagle, symbol of St John. On the south aisle wall is a brass with figures of Philip and Alice Williams in Elizabethan costume. At least four 16th century bishops were buried here but no monuments to any of them have survived.

MICHAELSTON-Y-FEDW *St Michael*

ST 241846

The wide 13th century nave and chancel form one block, although there is an original chancel arch between them. There are pilaster buttresses on the side walls, triple east lancets, and other single lancets in the side walls. Later 13th century additions are the south porch and west tower with an embattled parapet upon a corbel table. The tower doorway is a later insertion. A south chapel with a floor high above that of the church was added in the late 16th century. The font with a snake on the shaft and flowering foliage on the bowl is probably Norman, and there is a foliated cross slab plus a fragmentary pre-Reformation altar slab.

MITCHEL TROY *St Michael*

SO 493104

The fine chancel, aisled nave with three bay arcades having complex moulded piers, and the south porch are all 14th century. The aisle west lancets look older but are probably the same age as the rest. The tiny west tower has an inscription asking for prayers on behalf of Godfrey and Joanne, and was formerly dated 1414. The vestry was added during the heavy restoration of 1870-6 when the walls were refaced internally. There is a cup shaped Norman font. Adam of Usk was rector here in 1382, and Nathaniel Baxter was rector in 1602.

Mitchel Troy Church

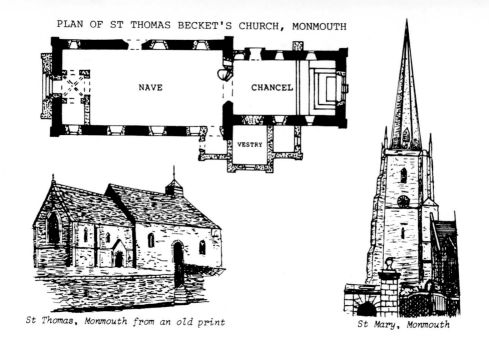

PLAN OF ST THOMAS BECKET'S CHURCH, MONMOUTH

NAVE

CHANCEL

VESTRY

St Thomas, Monmouth from an old print

St Mary, Monmouth

MONMOUTH *St Mary*   ST 509130

Only the 14th century west tower remains of the Benedictine priory church founded in c1080. The upper part and spire are of c1750 to a design by Nathaniel Wilkinson. The church itself was rebuilt in 1736-7 by Francis Smith and remodelled by Street in the 1880s. The heavy buttresses flanking the tower originally formed part of the 12th century west front. The north arcade was where the north wall now is, and the position of the south arcade is marked by a round respond now almost centrally placed on the inside of the west wall.

MONMOUTH *St Thomas Becket*   ST 505124

The suburb of Overmonnow, south of the town, was provided with its own church in the 1180s. The large unaisled nave and chancel each have original north doorways, that in the nave having several orders. The chancel arch is also original, although the jambs have been renewed, most of the windows renewed, and a new west front added.

MYNYDDISLWYN *St Tudor*   ST 194939

The church lies on a bare hilltop. The embattled tower with a NE stair turret, and perhaps also the six bay arcade, are 15th century. Otherwise the single chamber nave and chancel and the wide north aisle are mostly of 1820 and the late 19th century.

NASH *St Mary*   ST 344837

The spacious nave and chancel are probably slightly earlier than the late 13th century diagonally buttressed north transeptal tower. The spire may be later, and the other features and furnishings are 18th and 19th century. A roof mark on the tower shows there was a north aisle or chapel. A slot on one of the buttresses marks the height of the tide in the great flood of 1606.

NEWPORT *St Woolos*

A church was first established here in the early 6th century by a Welsh chieftain of Wentloog called Gwynllyw (Woolos in English). A later stone church was plundered in turn by Irish pirates, Danes, and the English under Harold Godwinson. It was destroyed by Caradoc, Lord of Caerleon, but was rebuilt after being granted by William Rufus to Gloucester Abbey. The nave built in c1120 was given new lancets in the 13th century, and has become a galilee chapel of St Mary. A very fine arch of c1180 with chevron ornamentation leads from it into a new aisled nave of five bays built in c1150-60.

After being burnt by Owain Glyndwr in 1402 the nave was rebuilt with wider aisles and a south porch. Henry VII's uncle Jasper Tudor, then Lord of Wentloog, was among those who contributed towards the addition of a west tower with diagonal buttresses and a polygonal NE stair turret. The south porch was rebuilt during the heavy 19th century restorations. In 1930 the church became the cathedral of the new Diocese of Monmouth. In 1960-2 the mostly rebuilt chancel was replaced by a longer new east end with spacious new vestries. The SE chapel is also of that build. The font is partly Norman. In niches in the galilee chapel are the effigies of Sir John Morgan of Tredegar, d1491, his wife Janet, and William Berkerolles' wife, c1226.

NEWCHURCH *St Peter*

The church commands wide views to the south. Restoration has left only a late medieval north doorway and porch, a tiny 14th century west tower with a later SE stair turret, the octagonal font, and the 17th century brass recording Elizabeth Harries' gifts to the poor.

OLDCASTLE *Dedication Unknown*

The rebuilding of 1864 by Seddon has left three Norman windows in the nave, a head on the chancel wall, and the tiny octagonal font.

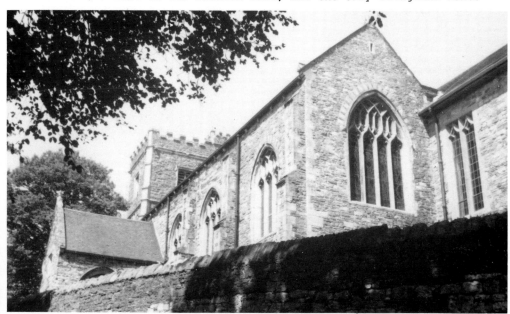

Cathedral Church of St Woolos, Newport

Penhow Church

PANTEG *St Mary*

The small tower with a NE stair turret is 15th century. The nave, four bay north aisle, chancel, and vestries are all 19th century.

PENALT *Dedication Unknown*   ST 523107

This interesting church is set high above the Wye. The nave north wall is 12th or 13th century and the saddleback roofed west tower is 14th century. The north windows, chancel, south aisle with four narrow arches on complex moulded piers and a squint to the chancel, and the south porch are all good 15th century work. Of that period also are the fine wagon roofs. The chancel arch is offset to the south allowing room for a doorway to the former roodloft from steps along the chancel north wall. There is an old chest. The main door dates from 1539 and has a heart on it. The only later features are a chancel north window, the three heavy buttresses against the nave north wall, and the Jacobean pulpit with pilasters, arches, etc.

PENHOW *St John The Baptist*   ST 424908

The church and castle lie together on a hill. Added to the Norman nave is a 13th century south tower with two bay arcades either side of it to short sections of aisle. There is a stone screen with two square openings either side of a pointed arch instead of a proper chancel arch. The chancel is mostly rebuilt but retails an original 13th century double piscina and a 14th century ogee headed recess. The porch adjoining the tower is 15th century.

PENRHOS *St Cadoc*   SO 416117

The nave has a 13th century south doorway and the chancel has two late 13th century cusped lancets. The priest's doorway, four south windows, another window re-set in the west wall of the aisle added in 1878, and the tower with a projecting bellstage are 15th century.

Pen-Y-Clawydd Church

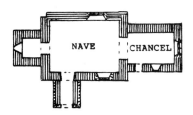

PLAN OF PEN-Y-CLAWYDD CHURCH

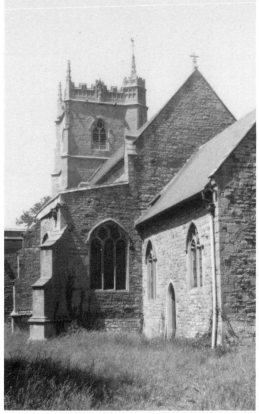

Peterstone Wentloog Church

PENTERRY   *Dedication Unknown*   ST 520988

This church lying alone in a field above the Wye is mostly rebuilt.

PEN-Y-CLAWYDD   *Dedication Unknown*   SO 452079

The pyramidal roofed west tower and small nave and chancel are all
probably 13th century. The nave has been slightly widened to the
north at some time, and the windows, low chancel arch, and timber
south porch are 19th century. On the porch floor is a worn floriated
cross slab of 1676. Beside the chancel arch is an equally worn 14th
century slab with a bust of a man emerging from a floriated cross.

PETERSTONE WENTLOOG   *St Peter*   ST 268801

This is a large and splendid 15th century church with a fully aisled
nave, large south porch, and diagonally buttressed west tower, but
the chancel and north aisle were rebuilt in the 19th century. The
aisles do not quite reach to the tower, leaving a very short section
of unaisled nave as in many Devon churches. The tower is embattled
with pinnacles at the corners. In niches in the parapet are figures
of St Mary, St James, St John, and St Peter. The arcade piers are
of a clustered type, and there is an old font. A stone on the chancel
exterior marks the height of the flood tide of January 20th, 1606.

41

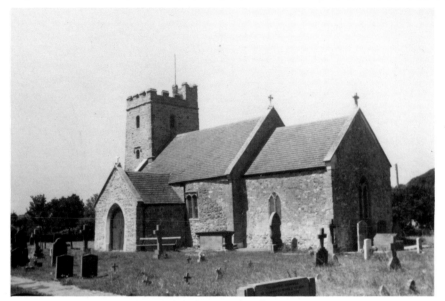

Portskewett Church

PORTSKEWETT *Dedication Unknown* ST 499882

Both the nave and chancel are 12th century, with a Norman window in
the chancel north wall, and a blocked doorway with a huge lintel in
the nave north wall. One south window with Y-tracery is of c1300,
and a nave south window, the small tower with a NE stair turret,
and perhaps the large south porch, are all 15th century.

RAGLAN *St Cadoc* SO 414076

In the very thick chancel south wall are two windows with tracery
of c1300. Some nave masonry may be 13th century, but the roodloft
staircase, windows, south doorway and porch, the north chapel with
a two bay arcade, and the embattled west tower with pinnacles are
all 15th century. The short north aisle dates from the Victorian
restoration when the windows were mostly renewed. The nave has a
fine coved roof, and contains a fragment of an old font. There are
two old chests, one dated 1677. The former roodloft staircase now
gives access to the pulpit. In the north chapel are the mutilated
effigies of William Somerset, 3rd Earl of Worcester, his son Edward,
4th Earl, and Elizabeth, wife of the latter, d1621. No monument of
Edward, 6th Earl, 2nd Marquess, d1667, also buried here, has survived.

REDWICK *St Michael* ST 413841

The chancel is 14th century and so probably are the nave and aisles
with three bay arcades. The east window has reticulated tracery.
The porch, which rises higher than the south aisle, the top storey
of the tower, and several windows are 15th century. The lower part
of the tower may be Norman. There are fleurons on the west doorway
arch soffit. There is a square 13th century font and a baptistry
of much later date for total immersion in the north aisle. One of
the three mass sundials on the porch marks the level of the flood
of 1606. Grotesque heads adorn the porch inner doorway. The church
was damaged by a German bomb during World War II.

ROCKFIELD *St Cenedlon* SO 487148

Only the octagonal font with blank traceried panels and the tower with a recessed timber upper stage survived a Victorian rebuilding.

ROGIET *Dedication Unknown* ST 457876

The tiny nave and the font are probably Norman. The 14th century chancel has an east window with reticulated tracery. The roodloft staircase, south doorway, and west tower are 15th century and the north aisle is Victorian. The tower has a SE stair turret with an octagonal top ending in a tiny spirelet.

RUNSTON *St Kenya* ST 495916

The village has gone leaving just one farm and the ruinous Norman chapel with a narrow chancel arch, north and south doorways, and several windows, all with rounded heads. There are footings of a west tower thought not to have been completed and superseded by a modest turret. The chapel fell into ruin in the late 18th century.

ST BRIDES NETHERWENT *St Bridget* ST 428896

Except for the saddleback roofed west tower and the font, the 13th century church was mostly rebuilt in the 19th century.

ST BRIDES WENTLOOG *St Bridget* ST 293824

The church, now disused and derelict, has a large nave with a north chapel opening off it by a now blocked two bay arcade, a chancel which is comparatively small, and a splendid diagonally buttressed west tower with richly panelled parapet having niches with statues of two saints, the Holy Trinity and the Virgin and Child. The four corner pinnacles have gone. All this is 15th century, with various original windows. Older only is the porch, perhaps 14th century, with what looks like a re-set Norman window above the outer arch.

Runston Chapel

43

Shirenewton Church

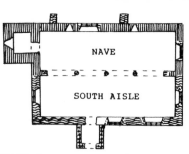

PLAN OF ST MAUGHAN'S CHURCH

■	12th Century
▥	13th Century
▨	14th Century
▧	17th Century
▦	18th Century
▒	19th Century

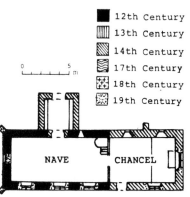

PLAN OF ST PIERRE CHURCH

ST ARVANS *St Arvan*   ST 517965

The Victorian restoration has left only the chancel of c1280-1300
with a shouldered lintelled priest's doorway and a two light window
and a 10th century cross fragment built into a north aisle window.

ST MAUGHANS *St Meugan*   SO 461171

The church is unusual for this part of Wales in having two naves,
i.e. two parallel bodies of equal width. The northern nave is 13th
century, having two north lancets. The tower with a timber framed
top to the west of it may also be 13th century. The 17th century
south nave has one original south window and an arcade of octagonal
timber pillars supporting a huge moulded beam. The south porch is
dated 1732 and the other windows are Victorian. The font is Norman.
On the chancel wall is a stone of 1740 with a tinted floral surround.

ST PIERRE *St Peter*   ST 515905

The church nestles beside the big house. It has one Norman window.
The north doorway and porch with a crocketted and pinnacled niche
over the outer arch, and the chancel with two original northern
windows are 14th century. The east and south windows are Victorian.
The nave has an old wagon roof. Of the 13th century are the font and
two graveslabs. One, to a priest, has a hand holding a floriated
cross on which are falcons, a lion and a dragon. The other is to
Urien St Pierre, d1239, with a cross, sword and French inscription.

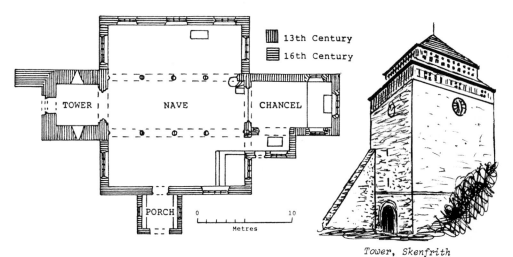

13th Century

16th Century

TOWER   NAVE   CHANCEL

PORCH

0 ——————————— 10

Metres

PLAN OF SKENFRITH CHURCH

Tower, Skenfrith

SHIRENEWTON *St Thomas Becket*   ST 478935

The nave, large south porch, central tower, and chancel are mostly
15th century. One tower window and the priest's doorway survived
the Victorian restoration when the north aisle was added. A tiger
head water spout appears on the west front and there are two human
headed gargoyles on the embattled parapet of the tower.

SKENFRITH *St Bridget*   SO 456203

The lower part of the west tower, the fully aisled nave with four
bay arcades and the chancel are all 13th century just as one might
expect with a major castle of that date nearby. The chancel arch is
decorated with dog-tooth ornament. The east and north windows are
14th century. Several windows are of the period 1480 to 1550 during
which the aisles were widened and covered with coved roofs, the
original chancel doorway was re-set in a tiny chapel added on the
south side, and a recessed timber framed upper stage and pyramidal
roof were added on the tower. In the north aisle are an altar tomb
with an incised slab depicting Sir John Morgan, d1533, and his wife
and family, and a red cope of embroidered velvet made in c1500. The
orphrey on the cope has figures of saints under canopies the hood
depicts the Virgin and child, three seraphim, and two double headed
eagles. Parts of the rood screen are re-used in the reader's desk.
The pulpit and chest are both dated 1661.

STANTON *Dedication Unknown*   SO 311213

A chapel of c1400 which served a grange of Llanthony Abbey has been
converted into a cowshed. Three ogival headed windows remain.

SUDBROOKE *Holy Trinity*   ST 507873

The Norman church below the bank of the camp is mostly reduced to
foundations except for the nave west wall with one lancet, the 13th
century chancel arch on plain imposts, and the arch of the later
medieval south porch. The chancel was enlarged in the 13th century.

Tintern Church

Grave Slab at St Pierr

TINTERN *St Mary*   ST 530099

A steep cobble path leads up to the ruined 13th century church high
above the village and abbey. Two windows and a niche survived the
drastic restoration of 1861-6, when the north tower was added.

TINTERN PARVA *St Michael*   SO 532007

The font is 13th century and so were the nave and chancel before
the 19th century restoration. The cross slab on the floor and the
south porch with roses on the vault, now a vestry, are 14th century.

TREDUNNOCK *St Andrew*   ST 380949

The small nave and chancel both have Norman windows. The west tower
and chancel arch are 14th century, and the priest's doorway, south
window, east window with fragments of old glass, and the SW porch
are 15th century. The porch outer archway is remarkably low. The
altar table of c1600 is panelled with flowers and flaming wheels,
and there are old pews and a font dated 1662 with a fluted bowl.
On the north wall is an interesting Roman tombstone dug up in 1680.

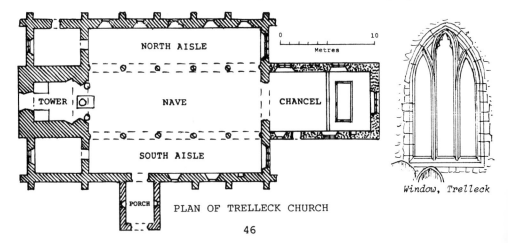

Window, Trelleck

PLAN OF TRELLECK CHURCH

Tredunnock Church

TREGARE *Dedication Unknown*   SO 417102

The nave and the chancel are both 13th century. The chancel arch
and three chancel windows are original; another window is dated
1638. Also 13th century, but obviously an addition, is the tower.
It is capped by a large weathercock. The ogee headed north window
and south doorway are 14th century, and the roodloft staircase, the
roof with embattled wall plates and ribs and bosses, and the south
windows and porch are 15th century. The east window is Victorian.

TRELLECK *St Nicholas*   SO 501055

Most of the existing church was erected after the Welsh burnt the
village in 1295. There are splendid five bay arcades with octagonal
piers, and clerestory windows above. The aisles embrace the west
tower although the latter has an arch towards the nave only. The
tower has a west window with reticulated tracery and a slightly
recessed and embattled top stage with a spire rising to 54m. There
are several orders of sunk quadrant mouldings on the west doorway.
Two north windows have cinquefoiled and trefoiled rere-arches but
most of the others are restored. In the south aisle is a piscina.
The chancel has been rebuilt but retains a re-set late 13th century
north window and a doorway of c1200. The south porch is 15th or
16th century and the south door bears the year 1595. In the south
aisle is a sundial dated 1640 and a small female effigy. There
are an elaborately carved chest, Elizabethan communion rails, fonts
of the pre-Norman, Norman, and later medieval periods, and a pulpit
dated 1640 which was originally a three decker.

TRELLECK GRANGE *Dedication Unknown*   SO 492017

The small rectangular chapel was mostly rebuilt in 1861.

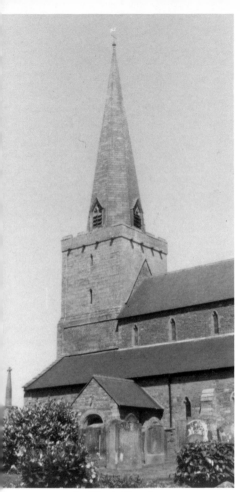

Trelleck Church   *Usk Priory Church*

TREVETHIN *St Cadoc*   SO 284020

Only the late 15th century ashlar faced tower with a NE stair turret
and an inscription to the ironmaster and M.P. Major John Hanbury,
d1734, survived the mid 19th century rebuilding of the church.

TROSTREY *St David*   SO 360044

The church lies alone high above the Usk. The single chamber and
west porch are 13th century although the battered oak screen with
a staircase to a former loft, several windows, and the roof with
bosses are 15th century. The porch has a stoup and an old roof. On
the west gable is a high double belcote. There is an old chest and
a pulpit with carved panels.

UDNY *St Mary*   ST 440869

The font and the nave with a round arched south doorway are Norman.
At the south end of the west wall is a 15th century doorway. The
porch is dated 1790 but may be older. All the windows are Victorian.

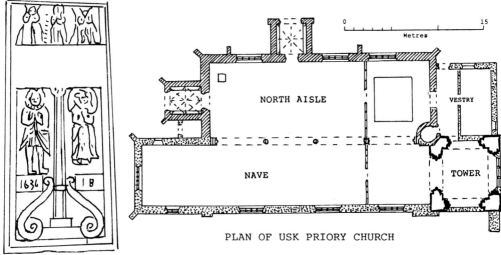

Grave stone at Trelleck

PLAN OF USK PRIORY CHURCH

USK *St Mary*   SO 379008

At the Dissolution the 12th century nave and central tower of the
Benedictine nunnery founded by Richard de Clare in c1135 were saved
for parochial use, three of the round arches under the tower being
blocked when the transepts and choir were destroyed. A vestry lies
on the site of the north transept. The three south windows and the
west bay of the nave are 19th century. The four bay arcade is 13th
century. The parishioners provided themselves with a wide new aisle
with west and north porches in the 15th century. The fine screen
closing off the east bay of both nave and aisle has vine patterns,
roses, foliage, and tracery. Fixed upon it is a brass commemorating
the celebrated chronicler Adam of Usk, c1365-1421. Other monuments
include that of a 17th century soldier who "did advance a pyke for
his Queene" and a scroll to Usk Grammar School founder Roger Edwards.

WHITSON *Dedication Unknown*   ST 381834

The south doorway with foliage capitals to the shafts and the font
with a band of lattice are Norman. The 15th century west tower has
a NE stair turret with a bee-hive like top. The porch outer arch
and most of the windows were renewed in the 19th century.

WOLVES NEWTON *St Thomas Becket*   ST 454998

The thin saddleback roofed west tower and the nave with one renewed
lancet are 13th century. A second south window, both nave doorways,
the south porch, and the chancel are 15th century. Several other
windows are Victorian. There are old altar rails in the chancel.

WONASTOW *St Wonnow*   SO 486107

The church lies hidden away beyond the house. The nave and chancel
are probably of 13th century origin but the chancel doorway and
windows with fragments of stained glass are 15th century, and the
chancel is a large cream-washed monument to George Milborne, d1637,
and his wife and family, and the nave contains an old altar table.

Baglan Church

GAZETTEER OF CHURCHES IN GLAMORGAN

ABERDARE   *St John The Baptist*   SO 000027

This plain church with a long nave and short chancel probably has mostly 12th century masonry although all the openings except perhaps the west lancet are Victorian. There is a square headed double bell-cote and a south porch of uncertain date.

BAGLAN   *St Baglan*   SS 753923

Further up the hill from the Victorian church is the ruined single chamber medieval church. It has a double belfry and 15th century east window, and a blocked 16th century three light south window.

BARRY   *St Nicholas*   ST 105673

The church was entirely rebuilt on a larger scale and on a different alignment in 1874-6, and the font taken off to All Saints' Church. The old building had a 13th century nave and chancel, a large 15th century porch, and a 16th century chancel arch. Parts of the porch and nave south wall were revealed by excavation in 1972.

BARRY ISLAND   *St Baruch*   ST 119666

In a wired-off enclosure beside the holiday camp entrance are the foundations of a tiny nave and apse of early date with a second building, probably a hermit's cell, close by on the north side.

BEDWAS   *St Barrwg*   ST 172892

The nave, which has a pointed south doorway approached by steps, the south porch, and the chancel are probably all 13th century. The saddleback roofed tower with gables facing north and south has a west doorway with a shouldered lintel suggesting a date of c1300. The vestry is Victorian. The church lies high on a slope above the Rhymney. Within it is a Norman font with a band of cable moulding.

BETTWS   *St David*   SS 899867

The round headed south doorway suggests that the nave masonry is Norman. The stoup in the porch looks 13th century and the shape of the priest's doorway suggests the chancel was rebuilt in c1480-1520.

PLAN OF BAGLAN CHURCH

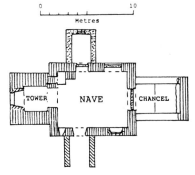

PLAN OF CAERAU CHURCH

Briton Ferry Church

BONVILSTON *St Mary*   ST 064741

In 1863 Pritchard and Seddon refaced the west side of the diagonally buttressed 15th century west tower and rebuilt most of the 13th century nave and chancel. However they left the chancel arch, rood stair in the nave SE corner, the two south doorways and the porch, and also some of the roof timbers, with heraldic shields. There are monuments to the Basset family in the chancel.

BRITON FERRY *St Mary*   SS 736943

At the west end of the short south aisle of the large aisled new church of 1891 is a small 16th century tower.

CADOXTON *St Cadoc*   ST 130693

The nave has a Norman north window but was mostly rebuilt in the 19th century. Another Norman window is re-set in the 15th century west tower built at the expense of the Andrews family of Cadoxton Court. The vaulted south porch is also 15th century. The piscina shaped like a column capital dates the widening of the chancel to the south to sometime in the 13th century.

CADOXTON-JUXTA-NEATH *St Catwg*   SS 756986

The nave and chancel were rebuilt in the 19th century when a north aisle and vestry were added, but the west tower is 13th century.

CAERAU *St Mary*   ST 135750

Beside an Iron Age hillfort overlooking one of Cardiff's western suburbs are ruins of a 13th century church with a small chancel and an almost square nave. The saddleback roofed west tower is 15th century and the vestry is Victorian. The vaulted south porch is now enclosed by boarding, the building having become a vandals' haunt.

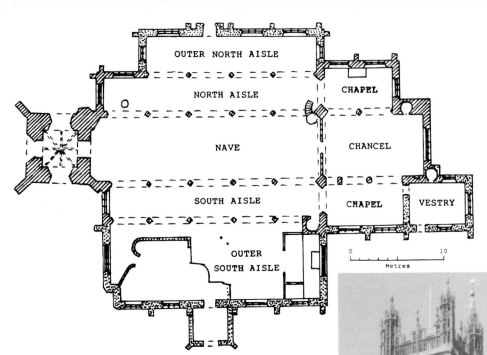

PLAN OF ST JOHN'S CHURCH, CARDIFF

CARDIFF *St John*   ST 183764

In the 1450s the original 12th century chapel was rebuilt with an aisled five bay nave and a three bay chancel flanked by two bay chapels. In the 1470s Anne Neville, wife of the Duke of Gloucester, later Richard III, commissioned John Hart to build the high west tower. It is similar to several Somerset towers, having a five light west window, diagonal buttresses, battlements and pinnacles with openwork, and a vaulted porch at the base. The church suffered a drastic restoration in 1852, and in 1889 the galleries inserted in 1813 were taken out and replaced by outer aisles. The south outer aisle is now mostly filled with modern vestries and offices. The north chapel has an old screen to the chancel and contains two Herbert effigies.

CARDIFF *St Mary*   ST 155803

Immediately south of the Norman borough lay a Benedictine priory founded by Robert Fitz-Hamon in the 1080s. In 1221 a parochial aisle was added, and other additions were made later. In the early 17th century Speed depicted it as a cruciform building with a central tower. It was then under threat of undermining by the Taff and the parish transferred to St John's. St Mary's collapsed c1670. Little now remains.

St John's Church, Cardiff

52

Coity Church

COITY
SS 924815

The cruciform church has a wide and thickly walled nave. The tower set over a vaulted crossing has later medieval belfry windows and may have been raised. The chancel, now painted blue inside, contains two small 14th century effigies to Turberville females and a 15th century chest carved with the symbols of The Passion. In the south transept is a tablet to Joan William, d1710.

COLWINSTON
SS 939755

The round Norman chancel arch is flanked by a pair of niches, one of which contains a medieval wall-painting. The chancel doorway and windows are 13th century and there is a male effigy in a niche. The east window, rood staircase, south porch and embattled western tower are all 16th century.

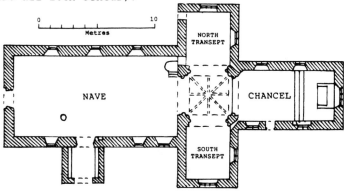

PLAN OF COITY CHURCH

53

Cowbridge Church

COWBRIDGE *Holy Cross*   SS 994746

As built in the 13th century to serve the newly founded town the church comprised a spacious nave, a central tower and a chancel. The tower has broaches to a smaller embattled octagonal top stage. The Llanquian aisle flanking the south side of the nave and tower, the nave west doorway, and the north chapel, now a vestry, are 15th century. The vestry east of the junction between the chancel and chapel, the rood staircase, and the large north window west of the Victorian porch are 16th century. On either side of the window can be seen the jambs of original lancet windows. The aisle arcade has piers of a quatrefoil section. A former spire is said to have been destroyed by lightning in 1480. In the aisle is a wall monument with kneeling figures of two 17th century carnes of Nash Manor.

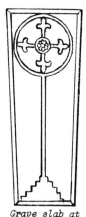

*Grave slab at
Eglwys Brevis*

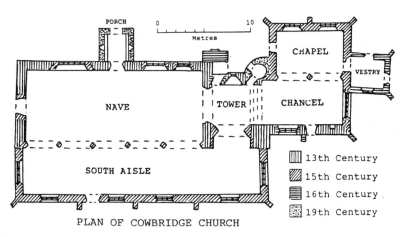

PLAN OF COWBRIDGE CHURCH

54

COYCHURCH *St Crallo*

SS 939797

Being larger than most of the surrounding medieval churches, this cruciform building of c1270-1300 is sometimes called 'The Cathedral of The Vale'. It has a long but comparatively narrow nave and aisles with four bay arcades upon octagonal piers and a low clerestory of cinquefoil windows. The nave west wall has a fine doorway below a three light window whilst the aisles have quatrefoil west windows. The central tower has a NW stair turret supported on a section of solid wall instead of a fifth arcade arch. The chancel and south transept were mostly rebuilt after the tower top collapsed in 1877. In the church is part of an 11th century preaching cross.

EGLWYS BREVIS *St Brice*

ST 006691

The name Brevis may refer to William de Braose. The arch between the 13th century nave and chancel was widened in the 15th century, when the rood stair was inserted. The porch outer archway is 16th century. The font is Norman, and there is a foliated cross slab and a stone commemorating Mary Bassa, who died in 1643 aged 12.

EGLWYSSILIAN *St Ilian*

ST 106890

The porch outer entrance is 13th or 14th century and the spacious nave probably has 13th century walling although the openings are all much later. The doorway and two windows are perhaps late 16th century and two south windows are dated 1759 and 1760. The west tower is of c1480-1520. The chancel was rebuilt in 1873.

EWENNY *St Michael*

SS 912778

This church served a Benedictine Priory founded in 1141 by Maurice de Londres as a cell of Gloucester Abbey. The nave of c1145 and the narrow north aisle added c1180 were used by the parish. After the Dissolution they were shortened at the west end, the aisle outer wall rebuilt, and a porch added. The central tower, transepts with pairs of eastern chapels and the barrel vaulted chancel became private property. Apart from the north transept and chapels these were still intact when they were opened to the public in 1949 as a state monument. The church lies within a circuit of 13th and 14th century precinct walls with towers and gateways. There are several Early Christian gravestones, effigies of the founder, c1200, and his son William, d1205, and Hawise de Londres, d1274, plus a large tomb of c1700.

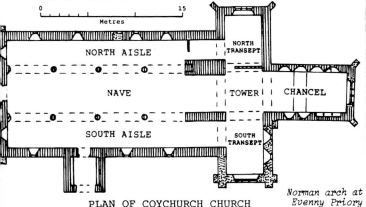

PLAN OF COYCHURCH CHURCH

Norman arch at Evenny Priory

Gileston Church

FLEMINGSTON *St Michael*   ST 016733

The church was very heavily restored in 1858 but originally the nave and chancel were 13th century and the south transept was added in the 14th century, no doubt at the expense of Joan le Fleming, whose effigy lies under the arch between transept and nave.

GELLIGAER *St Cattwg*   SO 136969

The spacious nave and chancel are probably of 13th century origin and the tower and porch are early 16th century, but all the windows plus the northern buttresses and vestries are Victorian.

GILESTON *St Giles*   ST 017671

The church was originally probably built in the 12th century but was almost entirely rebuilt in the 15th century when the porch was added. The chancel roof is of that period, and the screen, and the south door with the arms of those who paid for the rebuilding. There are several monuments to the Giles family, including one of 1724.

GLYNOGWR *Dedication Unknown*   SS 956872

The tower has belfry openings typical of c1480-1540. The chancel, nave, and south porch have old masonry but no ancient openings.

HIGHLIGHT *Dedication Unknown*   ST 707698

Foundations of the small 13th century church abandoned in the late 16th century were revealed by excavation in 1964-9. The chancel was built first as a self contained chapel, and the nave added later.

LALESTON *St David*   SS 875799

The nave masonry may be 13th century although the ogee-headed south doorway and porch, and the rood staircase, are of the 15th century when the chancel was rebuilt with a battered plinth and the lofty west tower added. the tower has a pair of two-light belfry windows facing west, an unusual arrangement, and gargoyles at the corners.

LISVANE *St Denys*   ST 192831

This 13th century church has a nave and chancel of equal width and a north transept with a short squint passage towards the high altar. Only one small window is original. The saddleback roofed west tower and the transeptal south porch are 16th century.

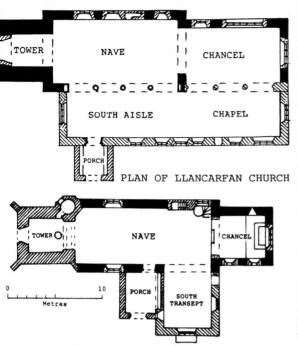

PLAN OF LLANCARFAN CHURCH

PLAN OF LLANBLETHIAN CHURCH

Llancarfan Church

LLANBAD *St Peter* SS 993853

This remote hill-top ruin was once a chapel-of-ease to Coychurch. The nave is 13th or 14th century and the chancel and south porch were later medieval additions. Regular services ended in 1812 and the building, then in a grove of pine trees, gradually decayed.

LLANBLETHIAN *St John The Baptist* SS 985740

The chancel has a Norman north window, two late 13th century south windows and a 15th century east window. The nave may be Norman but the late medieval rood stair with an old door still in situ is the only ancient feature. The 14th century south transept contains a tomb recess within which is now a male effigy found under the tower in the 19th century. In 1896 a crypt filled with 200 skeletons and 13th century tomb slab fragments was found beneath the transept. The diagonally buttressed west tower with an octagonal NE corner stair turret was added in the 1470s at the expense of Anne Neville.

LLANCARFAN *St Cadoc* ST 052703

The west tower with an original two-light belfry window, the nave, and the western part of the chancel north wall are Norman. A still earlier relic is part of a 9th century pillar cross now forming the sill of a south aisle window. A narrow south aisle with a four bay arcade was added in c1200-20. The doorway was re-set when the aisle was doubled in width and length in the 14th century. The eastern extension forms the Raglan chapel with its own three bay arcade to the chancel. The chapel has a decayed oak screen and there is also an oak chest. Of the 15th century are the tower west doorway and battlements, several north windows and the rood staircase, the roof and doorway of the chapel, and the remains of a former reredos.

LLANDOUGH *St Dochau*   SS 996729

The south doorway is of c1200. The window west of it is late 13th
century. The west window, south porch, rood staircase, nave roof,
and the small windows which lighted the screen are 15th century.
The chancel was rebuilt in 1869, when a vestry was added. There is
a brass depicting Wenllian Walshe, d1427, and a 14th century font.

LLANDOW *Holy Trinity*   SS 943734

The Norman nave has a round arched south doorway. The contemporary
chancel arch is pointed and is flanked by later niches. The chancel
with one lancet and the small saddleback roofed west tower are 13th
century. The priest's doorway, south porch, and a south window are
15th century. There is part of a 14th century female effigy inside.

LLANDYFODWG *Dedication Unknown*

The church contains a 14th century relief showing a pilgrim with a
Palmer's hat and the shell symbol of St James of Compostella.

LLANEDEYRN *St Edeyrn*   ST 221820

The south doorway and one small window on each side of the nave are
Norman. The chancel is the same width and has a 13th century north
window and priest's doorway. One nave window is 14th century. Two
others, plus the rood stair and south porch, are of about the same
period as the west tower which was dated 1521 on the west doorway.

LLANFRYNACH *St Brynach*   SS 979747

This building is currently little used. The nave and chancel may be
13th century in origin but the roof, rood staircase, and windows
are 15th century, as is the tower with a saddleback roof set within
a corbelled parapet. There are stone benches along the nave walls,
a rare survival. There is a font dated 1745 below the tower and a
pair of 17th century cross slabs to two of the Turberville family.

LLANGAN *St Canna*   SS 957778

The church was mostly rebuilt in 1856 and the only ancient feature
is the rood staircase door. In the graveyard are a 9th century wheel
cross showing Christ, and a 15th century cross with the crucifixion
and pieta, and six saints in niches.

LLANGEINOR *Dedication Unknown*   SS 924879

The nave and chancel are probably Norman as the south doorway has
a round arch, but all the windows are Victorian. The west tower
was added in c1480-1520. The church stands upon a high ridge.

LLANGYNWYD *St Cenydd*   SS 857887

The roll-moulded priest's doorway and one south lancet indicate the
13th century origin of the nave and chancel. One south window and
a small north window which lighted the screen, plus the west tower
with corner pinnacles are 15th century. Other windows are restored.

LLANILID *St Illtyd*   SS 977813

The unusual step-headed east window is the chief feature to see.
The tower, porch, two doorways, and most of the windows are of the
period c1480-1520, but the nave and chancel walls may be older.

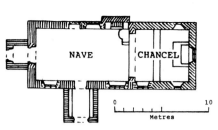

PLAN OF LLANSANNOR CHURCH

Llansannor Church

LLANILLTUD FAERDREF *St Illtyd*   ST 082866

The nave and comparatively small chancel are probably 13th century
in origin but lack ancient features. The saddleback roofed west
tower bears the date 1636 above the west doorway but is probably
older. The south aisle and vestries are additions of the 1980s.

LLANISHEN *St Isan*   ST 176818

The 13th or 14th century tower, nave, and chancel presently form
the south side of a large fully aisled 19th century church. The
old part has a porch and two chancel windows of the 15th century.

LLANMAES *St Cattwg*   SS 981694

The lofty west tower bears the date 1632 and the south windows of
the nave may be of the same period. The chancel was rebuilt in the
19th century when the porch and vestry were added. Inside are a
Norman font and an old screen with a faded painting of St george.

LLANMIHANGEL *St Michael*   SS 982719

The nave and chancel are 13th century, and the south windows and
the west tower are 15th century. A medieval cross-loop has been
re-set in the Victorian tower stair turret. In the nave is the tomb
chest of Criffith Grante, d1561, and on either side of the chancel
are 18th century monuments to the Edwins of Llanmihangel Place.

LLANQUIAN *St James*   ST 018744

Fieldwork by the R.C.A.H.M. has discovered that an outbuilding of
a farm on stalling Down is a much altered medieval chapel with the
unusual feature of an attached priest's dwelling at the west end.

LLANSANNOR *St Senwyr*   SS 994775

The east window and the doorways are of c1300. The rood staircase,
porch, chancel arch, west doorway, and a south window are of c1480-
1540, and the west tower with a four-gabled roof is probably still
later. Upon the south door is the year 1674. In the nave are some
monuments to the Truman family and a damaged wall-painting of St
Christopher discovered in the 1960s. In the chancel is a military
effigy probably of Gronw Ab Ifor.

LLANSAWEL *Dedication Unknown*   SS 763986

The nave and chancel are 13th century but the former was rebuilt in
the 19th century when a porch and south transept were added. The
16th century west tower has a stair turret at the NE corner.

Llantrisant Church

PLAN OF LLYSWORNEY CHURCH

NAVE · TOWER · CHANCEL · VESTRY

LLYSWORNEY CHURCH

0 _____ 10
Metres

- ■ 12th Century
- □ c1200
- ▥ 13th Century
- ▨ 14th Century
- ▧ 15th Century
- ▦ 19th Century

PLAN OF HEN EGLWYS, MARGAM

LLANTRISANT *SS Illtyd, Gwynno, Dyfodwg*   ST 046834

A large west tower with diagonal buttresses and a polygonal stair turret was added in c1480 to an aisled nave of uncertain date. The chancel and porch are further additions of c1600. The north porch, vestry, and the windows and buttresses are all 19th century.

LLANTRITHYD *St Illtyd*   ST 043727

The nave has windows, a doorway, and a porch of c1300. The north wall has been refaced. A Norman font lies outside near the 16th century west tower with a top stage rebuilt in 1711. The chancel was rebuilt in 1656, the year that appears over the stepped headed east window. Below the chancel carpet are hidden several incised slabs, including one to Robert de Rievaulx, Abbot of Margam, d1307. Another is dated 1586. There is also a tomb of 1597 with effigies of Sir Anthony Basset and his wife Elizabeth Mansel, a small figure of a 14th century civilian. and a 15th or 16th century screen.

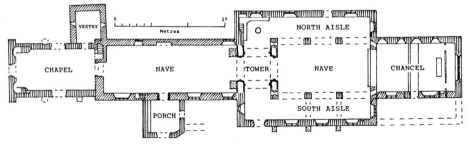

PLAN OF LLANTWIT MAJOR CHURCH

Mawdlam Church

LLANTWIT MAJOR *St Illtyd*   SS 966687

The school founded by St Illtyd here in c500 lasted until the 12th
century when a new church was built of which only the font and the
south doorway remain. A central tower was built east of the Norman
nave in c1200 and then in the late 13th century the latter became
incorporated into the west end of a new aisled nave of four bays
with a chancel and a south chapel serving a college of canons. The
original nave survived to serve the parish. To it a south porch and
a large west chapel, now roofless, were added in the 13th century.
In the 15th century the parish nave was rebuilt and a vestry added,
while the collegiate south chapel was pulled down and the arches to
it walled up. In the parochial nave are several cross fragments and
a foliated cross slab with a priest's head, and effigies of a 13th
century man and an Elizabethan woman. There are wall-paintings of
St Christopher and St Mary Magdalene, and a remarkable Jesse niche
in the south aisle, which also has flying arches inserted in 1905.

LLANWENSAN *Dedication Unknown*   ST 079793

A chapel with a Norman doorway tympanum in situ now forms a house.

LLANWONNO *St Gwynno*   ST 030956

The church is remotely sited in a forest high above the Hondda. The
walling is medieval but the south doorway is the only old opening.

LLYSWORNEY *St Tydfil*   SS 962741

This 13th century church has a plain central tower between the nave
and chancel with pointed arches offset to the north. Perhaps there
was originally a narrower Norman nave from which has survived the
ornamental stone now on the SE corner. The vestry with the tower
stair leading up from it is later medieval. In the nave are some
memorial tablets to the Carne family of Nash Manor.

61

MERTHYR MAWR

Doorway, Merthyr Mawr

Michaelston-Le-Pit Church

MARCROSS *Holy Trinity*   SS 925693

The chancel arch decorated with a roll-moulding and chevrons, and
the font are Norman. Of the 14th century are the saddleback roofed
west tower and the incised slab in a tomb recess in the nave, plus
the south doorway with leaf capitals. The porch is 19th century.

MARGAM *St Mary*   SS 802864 & 802866

The lengthy Norman abbey nave survives in parochial use but except
for the arcades was entirely rebuilt for Thomas Mansel Talbot in
1805-10. There are many Mansel monuments, including three alabaster
tombs and two wall-monuments. On a rock high above the abbey lies
a ruined 15th century chapel with remnants of fine windows.

MAWDLAM *St Mary Magdalene*   SS 806820

The west tower with open parapets on the side walls only, and the
nave are 13th century, and the west porch and tower arch are later
medieval. Below the tower is a Norman font. The chancel is rebuilt.

MERTHYR DYFAN *St Dyfan*   ST 115694

The nave and chancel are 13th century and have one original lancet
and a contemporary font. One north window may be 14th century. The
chancel roof, chancel arch, and the west tower are 16th century.

MERTHYR MAWR *St Roque*   SS 889781

On a wooded rock in the private grounds of Merthyr Mawr House is a
tiny 15th century ruined oratory with an original doorway, bellcote
and two windows surviving. Within it are fragments of older crosses.

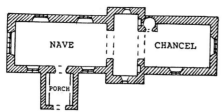

PLAN OF MICHAELSTON-LE-PIT CHURCH

Pendeyern Church

PLAN OF MONKNASH CHURCH

MICHAELSTON-LE-PIT *St Michael*   ST 152730

This church has a central tower between the nave and chancel with shallow transeptal altar recesses on either side. Several windows and the porch are 15th century, but the nave masonry may be older. Inside is the only three-decker pulpit in the Vale of Glamorgan.

MICHAELSTON-SUPER-ELY *St Michael*   ST 115763

The 14th century lancets of the nave and chancel were restored in the 1860s when a Norman chancel arch was replaced and the tower and the porch were added. In the tiny south transept is a 17th century monument to Iestyn ap Gwrgant, and in the chancel are 18th century tablets and other monuments to the Lewis family.

MONKNASH *St Mary*   SS 921705

Monknash belonged to Neath Abbey and has a Norman church with one original north window and a narrow round chancel arch. The north wall has been rebuilt with a batter, hiding traces of the blocked original north doorway. The porch is dated 1628 and the doorway and south windows may also be of that period or a little earlier.

NEATH *St Thomas*   SS 754977

Nothing remains of the late 12th century church. The diagonally buttressed west tower is Tudor and the nave is Late Georgian.

NEWCASTLE BRIDGEND *St Illtyd*   SS 903801

The nave and chancel were rebuilt in the 19th century when the aisle and vestry were added on the north side. However, there is a fine early 16th century west tower with gargoyles and low pinnacles.

NEWTON NOTTAGE *St John The Baptist*   SS 837775

The heavily buttressed 13th century west tower may have originally had a defensive function. The canopied tower doorway, the chancel, and the nave doorway and porch are all 15th century. One staircase served both the pulpit and the roodloft. The vestry was added in 1889. The church only attained parochial status in the 17th century.

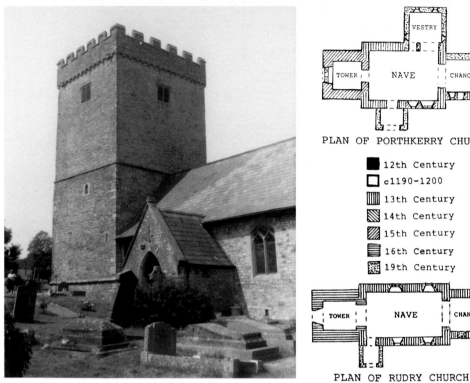

Pendoylan Church

PLAN OF PORTHKERRY CHURCH

■	12th Century
□	c1190-1200
▦	13th Century
▧	14th Century
▨	15th Century
▤	16th Century
▒	19th Century

PLAN OF RUDRY CHURCH

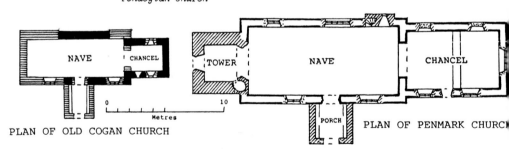

PLAN OF OLD COGAN CHURCH

PLAN OF PENMARK CHURCH

0   10
Metres

OLD COGAN *St Peter*   ST 168706

The small nave and chancel both have herringbone masonry of c1100.
The chancel has no east window but there are late medieval windows
in the side walls. The south porch, nave windows, and the whole of
the western third of the nave are of the 16th century.

PENDEYERN *St Cynoc*   SN 945086

The church has been mostly rebuilt except for the small west tower.

PENDOYLAN *St Cadoc*   ST 060767

The nave and chancel are mostly rebuilt except for the chancel arch.
The large and massive west tower is early 16th century.

Penmark Church

PENMARK *St Mary*   ST 058689

The round arched south doorway and the unmoulded pointed chancel arch with chevrons date the spacious nave and chancel to c1200. The font is slightly later and the west tower, the wagon roof over the nave, rood stair and one south window are 15th century. There was no east window prior to 1860. There are two monuments of the 1860s to members of the Lewis family. Both are made of alabaster.

PENRHYS *St Mary*

Penrhys was an important place of pilgrimage in the 16th century with a miracle-working image of the Virgin. Now only a short length of walling of the 13th century chapel lies near to a bus-stop.

PETERSTON-SUPER-ELY *St Peter*   ST 083764

The nave and chancel were mostly rebuilt in 1855 and 1891, leaving only the nave north wall and the 15th century west tower and font.

PICKETT *Dedication Unknown*   SS 927734

The small ruined single chamber retains no features of interest.

PORTKERRY *St Curig*   ST 083665

The nave and small chancel are 13th century. Several windows and the west tower are 15th century. There may once have been a north chapel. The porch is Victorian and the tower top stage was rebuilt in 1958. There is a monument to the physician Reynald Portrey, d1629.

PYLE *St James*   SS 825826

This 15th century church comprising a tower, nave, chancel, and a south porch was erected to replace a church at Kenfig engulfed by shifting dunes. Some of the features have been restored.

RADYR *Dedication Unknown*   ST 133802

The church has a 13th or 14th century tower but is otherwise rebuilt.

St Athan Church

Tomb Slab, St Bride's Major

RUDRY *St James*   ST 193865

The saddleback roofed west tower has a round arched west doorway,
perhaps of c1500 rather than c1200. The only pre-Victorian feature
of the small nave and chancel is a 14th century north window.

RUMNEY *St Augustine*   ST 215791

The very long nave has a battered base to the north wall. Probably
it dates from c1200. A doorway of that period is re-set in the 13th
century west tower. The tower top and one chancel window are 15th
century but the chancel is otherwise mostly rebuilt, and the nave
windows and north vestries are 19th century.

ST ANDREWS MAJOR *St Andrew*   ST 138715

The south doorway and the walls of the nave and chancel are 13th
century. The church was remodelled in c1480-1520 when the high west
tower, the porch, the wide north aisle with a four bay arcade, and
a north chapel were added. The latter has been rebuilt to serve as
a vestry. The font is Norman.

ST ATHAN *St Tathan*   ST 017680

The nave has a 14th century doorway and the chancel has a row of
13th century lancets. The central tower with plain pointed arches
and the transepts may be 13th century also but the chief features
of interest are the tombs with effigies of Sir William Berkerolle,
d1329, and his wife Phelice de Vere, and Sir Roger Berkerolle, d1351,
and his wife Katherine Turbeville. The porch is 15th century and
the east window dates from the restoration of 1888.

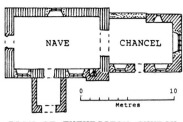

PLAN OF TYTHEGSTON CHURCH

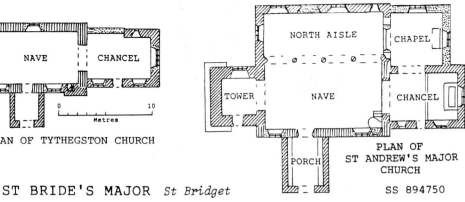

PLAN OF
ST ANDREW'S MAJOR
CHURCH

ST BRIDE'S MAJOR *St Bridget*   SS 894750

The porch and nave windows are Victorian but the masonry may be of
the time of the Norman chancel arch. The 13th century chancel is
long like the nave and has three renewed south lancets and a large
15th century plain mullioned north window which lights a recess in
which is the tomb chest of John Butler, d1460, and Jane Bassett.
They probably paid for the big west tower with diagonal buttresses
and a SE stair turret with cross loops with oilets.

ST BRIDE'S-SUPER-ELY *St Bridget*   ST 097776

The Norman nave and chancel are heavily restored, the chancel arch
being renewed in 1849 and the porch outer entrance transferred from
Margan Abbey. The font is 14th century and there is a saddleback
roofed tower of uncertain date. The tablet to Captain William Jones,
d1658, and his sons came from the demolished chapel of Llanfair Fawr.

St Bride's-Super-Ely Church

St Bride's Major Church

St Fagans Church

ST DONATS *St Donat*   SS 933681

The chancel arch and font are Norman and there was once an apse.
The porch and tower are 13th century, the Stradling chapel is 14th
century, and the chancel and several nave windows are 15th century.
In the chapel are marble monuments to Sir Edward Stradling, d1609,
and his wife Agnes, Sir Thomas Stradling, d1738, and a set of panels
to various members of the family painted by Byrd in the 1590s.

ST FAGANS *St Mary*   ST 122772

Excavations in 1979 in the museum grounds revealed the footings of
the original parish church dedicated to St Fagan which was still
standing in 1538. From it have come the Norman stones re-set in the
doorways of the present 14th century parish church. The chancel has
fine sedilia but was heavily restored by Street in 1860, when the
north aisle was added. The tower, porch, and font are 15th century.
Inside are several monuments to the Plymouth family.

ST GEORGES *St George*   ST 105766

This is a small 14th century cruciform church with a central tower
which has the arms of Iestyn ap Gwrgant on the boss of the crossing
vault. There is an elaborate cusped tomb recess in the north wall
of the chancel. The 15th century font has blank quatrefoils. The
existing north transept and the four-gabled tower top are of 1838.

St Georges Church

PLAN OF ST DONATS CHURCH

68

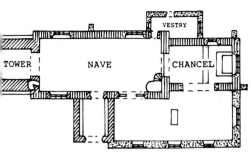

PLAN OF ST NICHOLAS CHURCH

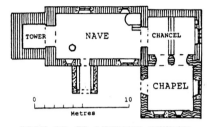

PLAN OF ST LYTHANS CHURCH

St Mellons Church

ST HILARY *St Hilary*   ST 016733

The priest's doorway and two small windows indicate that the nave and chancel are Norman. The south aisle is Victorian but has a 14th century arcade and a re-set doorway of c1200. The fine diagonally buttressed west tower is 15th century. There are effigies of Thomas Basset, d1423, and a man of the de Cardiff family in civilian dress.

ST LYTHANS *St Bleddian*   ST 111729

The saddleback roofed tower, nave, and chancel are all probably 13th century. The font is Norman. The 17th century Button chapel on the south side has a rustic arcade. The east window is 19th century.

ST MARY HILL *St Mary*   SS 957793

The former round Norman chancel arch now forms a rere-arch to one of the north windows. Otherwise the tower, nave, and chancel were rebuilt in 1884 except the double piscina and priest's doorway.

ST MELLONS *St Mellon*   ST 228814

The small chancel and the long wide nave have their south walls in line with each other. So the latter must have been widened. The 13th century tower with a 15th century top lies in the middle of the south side. West of it is a big porch and east of it an aisle with two 14th century arches to the nave and one to the chancel. All the windows and the vestry are Victorian but there are old roofs on the nave and porch. Inside is a small 15th century octagonal font.

ST NICHOLAS *St Nicholas*   ST 090744

The tower, nave, chancel, and south porch are mostly 15th century. The Victorians extended the transept east of the porch eastwards. There is a 13th century font.

Welsh St Donats Church

SULLY *St John The Baptist* ST 152684

A Norman chancel arch and a 15th century south aisle and porch are said to have been removed in the early 19th century. So the late medieval south windows must be re-set. The nave now has no doorway entrance being by a doorway dated 1701 in the 15th century tower.

TYTHEGSTON *St Tydwg* SS 858788

The west doorway, porch, and chancel features are of c1450-1520, but the nave doorway is earlier. A north chapel has been removed.

VAYNOR *St Gwynno* SN 049104

Near the church of 1870 is a ruinous small single chamber medieval church with a 16th century tower inserted into the west end of it.

WELSH ST DONATS *St Donat* ST 027763

The tower base, nave and chancel, and font are all 13th century. The porch is 14th century, several windows and the nave roof are 15th century, and the upper parts of the tower are 16th century.

WENVOE *St Mary* ST 123726

The tower was rebuilt in 1699 and the nave and chancel features are of 1876. In the nave are monuments to the Thomas's of Wenvoe Castle.

WEST ABERTHAW *Dedication Unknown* ST 024667

The R.C.A.H.M. recently discovered a cattle shed at West Aberthaw to be a medieval chapel with two blocked windows and a piscina.

WICK *St James* SS 924722

The rebuilt nave was originally Norman like the narrow round chancel arch flanked by two smaller openings. The saddleback roofed tower is perhaps also Norman. The chancel features are 16th century.

Cheriton Church

Ilston Church

GAZETTEER OF CHURCHES IN GOWER

BACKINSTON *Dedication Unknown*   SS 576881

In a field is the ivy mantled ruin of a tiny chapel measuring just 5.6m long by 3.6m wide externally. The doorway is the only feature.

BISHOPSTON *St Teilo*   SS 578893

The tower, nave, and font are all Norman, and the chancel is 13th century with an original doorway and side windows. Two nave windows are 14th century, two others are 15th century, and three more plus the tower battlements and the south porch are 19th century.

BURRY HOLMS *St Cennydd*   SS 401926

On an island beyond Llangenneth Burrows are the remains of a small Norman chapel. The tiny square chancel has replaced a former apse.

CASWELL *St Peter*   SS 590883

The east gable with the outline of a large window and foundations of the side walls lie hidden in foliage in a valley near Bishopston.

CHERITON *St Cadoc*   ST 450932

This is a comparatively unaltered 13th century church comprising a nave, central tower, and square chancel. There are several lancets, plus a 15th century east window and some fine later furnishings.

CWRT-Y-CARNE *St Michael*   SN 573004

Little remains of this chapel in marshland beside Loughor estuary. It was a grange of Neath Abbey and was probably Norman with a later porch. The ruined walls were still almost intact as late as 1899.

ILSTON *St Illtyd*   SS 553894

The nave is Norman and has original north and south doorways. The outer porch entrance also looks Norman but is probably much later. The barrel vaulted south transeptal tower and the chancel with a shallow recess in the north wall and a plain pointed arch to the nave are 13th century. There is a later south chapel, and the nave has an old roof. Nearby are remains of what is said to have been the first Baptist chapel in Wales (1649) near to a well-chapel site.

Llandeilo Tal-Y-Bont Church

Llangenneth Church

Llanrhidian Church

KNELSTON *St Mary*   SS 468890

Beyond a farm near Knelston school are footings of a small chapel.

LLANDDEWI *St David*   SS 460890

The tiny **saddleback** roofed tower with east and west parapets only,
and the **chancel entered** through a plain pointed arch with a slight
chanfer **are out of axis with,** and probably slightly later additions
to, a nave of c1180-1200 containing a plain tub font. The porch and
one small **window in each** nave side wall are 14th century. Several
other windows are 19th century.

LLANDEILO TAL-Y-BONT *St Teilo*   SN 585030

Little remains on site for the ruin has been removed for eventual
reconstruction at the St Fagans Welsh Folk Museum. It comprised a
13th or 14th century nave and chancel to which a south aisle and
porch, and a north chapel were added in the 15th century. The east
wall was later rebuilt and new side windows provided. In the 1980s
wall paintings of c1500 with various saints were discovered.

LLANGENNITH *St Cenydd*   SS 428914

St Cenydd founded a church here in the 6th century. The monastery
was destroyed by the Danes in 986 and the church was rebuilt in the
12th century by Henry de Newburgh. Of it there remain the slightly
later north transeptal tower with a saddleback roof and a round
arch on plain imposts which led to a chapel, or perhaps the Norman
nave. The large new nave, chancel and north porch built in the 13th
century made this the largest Gower church east of Oystermouth. The
east window is 14th century. There are three incised coffin lids
and the mutilated effigy of a knight.

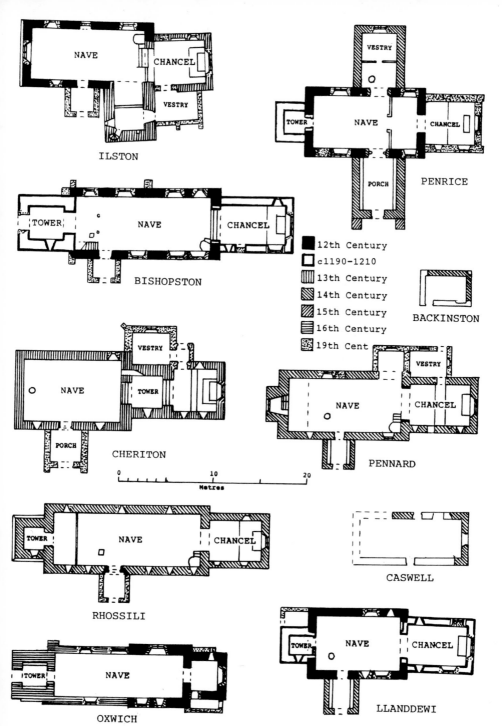

ILSTON

PENRICE

BISHOPSTON

BACKINSTON

12th Century
c1190-1210
13th Century
14th Century
15th Century
16th Century
19th Cent

CHERITON

PENNARD

0   10   20
Metres

RHOSSILI

CASWELL

OXWICH

LLANDDEWI

PLANS OF GOWER CHURCHES

73

Oxwich Church

Oystermouth Church

LLANGYFAELACH *St Cyfelach* SS 646990

The church itself was demolished after storm damage in 1803 leaving only the tower with a plain pointed arch of c1200. Above the north door is a 7th or 8th century cross stone. A 10th century cross base lies nearby and another cross lies within the 19th century church.

LLANMADOC *St Madoc* SS 439935

The tiny saddleback roofed tower with parapets only on the side walls, and the nave with a round arched doorway are probably both Norman. The chancel and south porch are 19th century.

LLANRHIDIAN *SS Illtyd & Rhidian* SS 496922

The nave is entirely rebuilt but the chancel may have 13th century walling and there is a splendid late medieval west tower with a SE stair turret. In the porch is the 9th century 'leper stone' with elementary human figures and animals carved upon it.

NICHOLASTON *St Nicholas* SS 513884

The 14th century church was mostly rebuilt in 1894.

OXWICH *St Illtyd* SS S05861

The more thickly walled eastern half of the nave and the very tiny chancel formed a Norman chapel. One south window may be 14th century and the west part of the nave and the west tower are 16th century.

The Tower, Llangyfelach

Pennard Church

OYSTERMOUTH *All Saints*   SS 616880

The tower, long nave, and chancel are all probably of 13th century origin although the tower top and several windows are late medieval. The chancel has three east lancets and contains a pillar piscina. It and the nave now form a south chapel and aisle to a large new late 19th century church. There is a scalloped Norman font.

PENMAEN *St John The Baptist*   SS 532887

The foundations of the original Norman nave and chancel church out among the dunes were excavated in 1860, but are now hard to find. The new church built in the 14th century has been mostly rebuilt. Two grave slabs, one of 1675, are the only features of interest.

PENNARD *St Mary*   SS 545855 & 566887

Near the castle is a defaced fragment and foundations of the Norman church engulfed by sand in the 14th century when the present church was built. It is almost the same size and incorporates the round chancel arch and other features of the older building. The porch and diminutive tower upon a thickened west wall are 15th century. The north transept and north vestry are 19th century.

PENRICE *St Andrew*   SS 493879

The tower, nave, and chancel arch are Norman. The chancel has been mostly rebuilt and the nave has Victorian windows whilst the tower has a late medieval top. One of the 14th century transepts forms a porch with an oak framed doorway set within an arch to the nave.

PORT EYNON *St Catwg*

SS 466854

The nave, chancel, and north transept are mostly rebuilt. The porch and inner doorway plus one south lancet are the only ancient features.

REYNOLDSTON *Dedication Unknown*

SS 479900

Only a medieval font has survived the 19th century rebuilding.

RHOSSILI *St Mary*

SS 417881 & 414883

The original Norman church engulfed by the dunes was excavated a few years ago and simple painted patterns were discovered on the walls. The long low 14th century church with a saddleback roofed tower in the middle of the village has a fine Norman south doorway with side shafts, chevrons, and dogtooth on the hoodmould. It may have originally formed the chancel arch of the church in the dunes.

SWANSEA *St Mary*

SS 656929

Hardly any medieval work remains in the church on account of very extensive 19th century rebuilding and bomb damage in 1941 when the fine ornamental 16th century tomb of Sir Matthew Craddock suffered destruction. The church has a wide fully aisled nave and a south transeptal tower plus various chapels and vestries flanking the chancel. The chief treasure now is the fine late 15th century brass with figures of Sir Hugh Johnys of Llandimore and his wife Maude.

Penrice Church

Rhossili Church

FURTHER READING

The Royal Commission on Ancient and Historical Monuments has yet to publish volumes about medieval churches and castles in Glamorgan and Gwent, nor have the Buildings of Wales volumes for those areas yet appeared, so there are big gaps in the information available.

Medieval Churches of The Vale of Glamorgan, Geoffrey Orrin, 1988
Lost Churches of Wales and The Marches, P. Davis & S. Lloyd Fern, 1990
A Guide to Welsh Parish Churches, R.W.Soden, 1984
The Companion Guide to South Wales, P.Howell & E.Beazley, 1977
The Towns of Medieval Wales, Ian Soulsby, 1983
A History of The County of Glamorgan, Vol III, 1971
A History of Monmouthshire (several vols) Sir Joseph Bradney
Monmouthshire (King's England series), Arthur Mee
Periodicals Morganwg, Gwent Local History, Archeologia Cambrensis.